# EARLY MEDIEVAL PHILOSOPHY

# EARLY MEDIEVAL
# PHILOSOPHY

### GEORGE BOSWORTH BURCH

FLETCHER PROFESSOR OF PHILOSOPHY
TUFTS COLLEGE

## King's Crown Press

COLUMBIA UNIVERSITY, NEW YORK

PUBLISHED IN GREAT BRITAIN, CANADA, AND INDIA
BY GEOFFREY CUMBERLEGE, OXFORD UNIVERSITY PRESS
LONDON, TORONTO, AND BOMBAY

MANUFACTURED IN THE UNITED STATES OF AMERICA

# PREFACE

WHEN Peter Abelard resolved to "desert the court of Mars for the bosom of Minerva," he was following the conviction that philosophy is the field in which a rational being should contend. In spite of censorship and loyalty probes, he succeeded in living the life of a scholar who followed truth as he saw it, both as an end in itself and as a means by which man acknowledges his Creator and comes to know himself. This book is dedicated to his memory and is intended for those who, in this new age of military crusades and thought control, still look to truth as the force which keeps them free.

The early Middle Ages, a sort of neo-pre-Socratic period, displayed a spontaneity and diversity of thought which continued until the thirteenth-century revival of Aristotle gave scholars an accepted canon of philosophical terminology. This book describes the doctrines of five outstanding philosophers of that period. As it is based entirely on the sources, the author hopes that it contains no gross errors of fact, at least within the limits set by the extent of the sources available, but he cannot hope that there will be complete agreement as to which philosophers of the period are the most interesting or significant. In any case, the historian of philosophy can only follow where the paleographer has led the way. The most important recent contribution to the study of early medieval philosophy has been the publication by Bernhard Geyer of certain previously unpublished logical works of Abelard. Excellent editions of Anselm and Bernard have long existed. Among the greatest needs now are the preparation of a critical text of Erigena and a search for unpublished works of Isaac of Stella.

The author is indebted to Dr. John Goheen for first suggesting this work, to Dr. Étienne Gilson for assistance with certain parts of it (as well as for much of his knowledge of medieval philosophy in general, obtained from that great teacher through books, lectures, and conferences), to Mrs. James H. Woods for many valuable criticisms, to Dr. John Wild for certain suggestions, to the late Dr. Erich Frank for criticizing the manuscript, and to Dr. Betty B. Burch for active collaboration in every stage of the work.

He is also indebted to the Harvard University Press for permission to reprint the section on Isaac of Stella's ontology, which is substantially identical with Appendix A to his edition of Bernard of Clairvaux's *Steps of Humility*.

Readers who wish to study the sources will find that the following are the works of greatest philosophical interest by the writers discussed in this book: Erigena's *Division of Nature;* Anselm's *Monologion* and *Proslogion;* Abelard's *Christian Theology, Introduction to Theology, Know Thyself,* and gloss on Porphyry in *Logic "Ingredientibus";* Bernard's *Steps of Humility, Loving God, Grace and Free Choice,* Letter 18, Sermon 3 for Whitsunday, Sermon 4 for All Saints', Sermons *De diversis* 6, 32, 45, and Sermons on Canticles 5, 23, 31, 36, 50, 62, 71, 74, 80, 81, 83, 85; and Isaac's *The Soul* and Sermons 19–25.

G. B. B.

Tufts College
April 21, 1950

# CONTENTS

# Chapter I. JOHN SCOTUS ERIGENA

## THE STUDY OF NATURE

NATURE (*natura, φύσις*) was the principal object of study for most ancient philosophers. While they did not neglect the study of man and the ways by which he knows nature, they did not, like many modern philosophers, consider the theory of knowledge the principal problem of philosophy. More interested in the object of knowledge than in its method, they thought of man as part of nature, not of nature as part of human experience. Their problem was the problem of being, to know what is the most real aspect of things, what is that which truly is.

The most ancient western philosopher whose works have survived is Plato. There were others before him, but their writings have been lost. One of these earlier philosophers, Democritus, is said to have found the fundamentally real nature in the invisible material atoms of which visible things are made, the visible forms being mere transient groups of atoms. The philosophy of Plato was diametrically opposed to this materialism. According to him, the real nature is found in the eternal ideas which are the archetypes according to which material things are formed. While it had long been a principle of the ancient Babylonian wisdom that terrestrial things are copies of eternal archetypes existing in heaven, Plato developed this principle in an idealistic sense, maintaining that the eternal archetypes are not the visible constellations but the intelligible ideas, of which even the constellations, the most beautiful things in the visible world, are imperfect copies. All things which are apprehended by the senses come into being and pass away; but those things which are apprehended by the understanding are eternal and therefore truly real.

In the long line of philosophers who followed Plato and developed his philosophy the most important were Aristotle and Plotinus. Aristotle described the organon or system of logic by which nature can be apprehended rationally. He distinguished the ten categories into which all beings can be grouped—essence, that which a substance is in itself, so as to be able to exist by itself, and the nine kinds of accidents, which are not essential to the substance of which they are predicated. He taught that any substance has both form and matter, and that therefore an immaterial form is no more substantial than unformed matter. His doctrine, if not contradicting Plato's, was marked by a greater interest in the visible world of particular substances existing in time and space. Plotinus, on the other hand, was interested rather in the pure ideas. He taught that these exist eternally in the divine mind. This mind is an emanation from the one true being, which is apprehended only in mystical ecstasy, and from this mind emanates the cosmic soul which animates the world.

Meanwhile a new basis for philosophy had been given by the teaching of Jesus, who amazed the world by his life and by his doctrine, speaking *as by authority, and not as the scribes*. The Gospels tell us relatively little of his own teaching, but the Church founded by his disciples had a definite doctrine. It taught that God, the eternal being, is one essence in three substances, as the Greeks said, or one substance in three persons, as the Latins said—the two phrases meaning the same thing; these persons are the Father, the Son or Word begotten by the Father, and the Holy Ghost proceeding from the Father through the Son or from the Father and the Son—all equally God and eternal; God created the world from nothing; he created man in his own image, but man fell into sin and became separated from God; the Word became man, was born as Jesus Christ, who was both God and man, sacrificed himself at the crucifixion to redeem man from sin, and rose again in triumph over death; those who by free will cooperating with God's grace free themselves from sin will be rewarded after the end of the world by eternal life in their resurrected bodies and by the vision of God which is man's greatest good.

Substituting the word *God* for the word *nature* did not solve the problem of being or of the relation between the eternal and the visible. But philosophy, enriched and inspired by the Christian revelation, progressed with new vigor. The most important Christian philosophers of the patristic period were, among the Greeks, Origen and Dionysius, and among the Latins, Augustine. Origen, a contemporary of Plotinus, taught that God is eternal, is a spirit, and is goodness; therefore all his creatures are created eternally, are spirits, and are good. Evil is nothing but the absence of God; matter is nothing but the absence of spirituality which results from the absence of God. Some created spirits have turned away from God and so fallen into material bodies, which are unreal and therefore mortal. But they are able, with God's assistance, to return to him and thus restore the complete spirituality of the world. Dionysius, that is, the unknown fifth or sixth-century theologian whose works were attributed to St. Paul's disciple Dionysius the Areopagite, attempted to give the truest possible description of God. This is done in two ways. The positive way affirms of God all positive attributes, because he, as the cause of all things, may be said in a transcendent sense to be all things. The negative way denies of God all attributes whatever, even being, because he transcends all our concepts, and so is absolutely nothing conceivable. Augustine, who after his conversion to Christianity became the most powerful champion of orthodoxy against various heresies, emphasized the implications of the original sin by which humanity turned away from God. By his own free choice of evil man fell from his original state of innocence into his present state of sin. Although he retains perfect freedom of choice, he cannot rise again without assistance, because the sinful nature naturally makes sinful choices. He needs the aid of God's grace, not only in order that his merits may be rewarded, but even in order that he may have any merits to reward. Consequently, while all men are saved or damned in accordance with the merits of their own free choices, only those whom God has predestined to receive his grace actually deserve, and so attain, salvation, all others being justly damned for their sins. Since the sinful state which prevents man from willing the good likewise prevents him from knowing the truth, he is dependent for knowledge also on the divine grace of revelation, and must believe in order to understand.

## JOHN SCOTUS ERIGENA

These philosophers, together with many others, made their several contributions to philosophy, and by these contributions a profound comprehension of nature was gradually developed in the ancient world. The general agreement among them was not obscured by the many differences of detail. But none of them ventured to synthesize the various doctrines into a harmonious whole which should exhibit the entire system of nature as understood by the philosophers. Such a synthesis was made by John Scotus Erigena. He also had original contributions to make. But his work appears primarily as a work of synthesizing, in which many of the most profound intuitions of the pagan and Christian philosophers find their place in a unified scheme of nature.

John Scotus Erigena lived in France in the middle of the ninth century. Little is known of his life. He is believed to have been a native of Ireland and to have studied there before coming to France. He occupied the chair of Alcuin as head of the Palace School, and he was a personal friend of the king Charles the Bald, who admired his erudition and his skill at repartee. His reputation for learning was well founded. He studied both the Latin and the Greek Fathers of the Church. This in itself was extraordinary, for at that period Greek was very little read even among persons who pretended to be educated. He took part in the theological controversies of the time, concerning predestination and the eucharist, his contributions being remarkable for their brilliance rather than for their orthodoxy; concerning the former he maintained that there is a predestination to good but not to evil; concerning the latter, that the body of Christ is truly present in the sacrament—but not the physical body; these doctrines followed as corollaries from his philosophy. There is a story that he was summoned to England by Alfred the Great and taught at Malmesbury, where his students were so critical of his lectures that they stabbed him to death with their pens.

Among his scholarly works was a translation from Greek into Latin of the four books of Dionysius—the *Celestial Hierarchy,* the *Ecclesiastical Hierarchy,* the *Divine Names,* and the *Mystical Theology*—together with his ten letters. Their attribution to the disciple of St. Paul endowed these books with an authority second only to that of the Bible, and they had a considerable influence in the later Middle Ages. He also wrote a commentary on the *Celestial Hierarchy*—a very useful supplement, for his literal translation, retaining the Greek idiom, is almost unintelligible. Other extant works include a translation of the *Ambigua* of Maximus the Confessor, a homily on the prologue to the Gospel of John, a book on predestination, and several poems in elegiac meter; and still other works have been attributed to him.

His great masterpiece, however, was his book on metaphysics entitled the *Division of Nature.* Synthesizing as it does the philosophical accomplishments of fifteen centuries, this book appears as the final achievement of ancient philosophy. It is written in a clear and facile Latin, without literary pretensions, and has the form of a dialogue between Master and Disciple. The philosophy presented is definitely a system, but there is little system in the presentation. Erigena, like Augustine, followed in his writing not the "order of reason" but the "order of charity," which requires constant digression in order that no important point may be left unexplained.

In the *Division of Nature* Erigena appears uncompromisingly as a rationalist. It is by reason, and only by reason, that we comprehend nature. But his rationalism does not imply, as in the case of Descartes or Spinoza, a confidence in his ability to fathom all the secrets of nature by his own unaided ratiocinations. Erigena is much more modest. He does not believe either that "good sense is of all things the most equally distributed" or that he is himself unusually well endowed with it. He seeks truth by studying the writings of the Fathers; his actual source of knowledge is authority rather than reason. But there is no opposition between the two. Not only does true authority harmonize with right reason, since both flow from the same font of divine wisdom,[1] but authority is authoritative only because it is rational. Reason is eternal, and so prior by nature to authority, which is temporal. Authority proceeds from true reason, but reason never proceeds from authority. Authority which is not approved by reason is invalid, but reason depends on its own strength and needs no support from authority. Authority is "nothing except truth discovered by the force of reason and written down by the holy Fathers for the use of posterity." [2] We follow the authority of the Fathers because we recognize that they were wiser, that is, more rational, than we. To approve our own ideas and disapprove those of others, is most dangerous, prideful, and contentious.[3] "It is not for us to judge the understandings of the holy Fathers, but to adopt them with piety and reverence; nevertheless we are not forbidden to choose that which seems, by consideration of reason, to accord best with the divine scriptures." [4] Authority is the source of knowledge, but our own reason remains the norm by which all authority must be judged. It must decide what is the true authority; and any doctrine which is repugnant to reason is unhesitatingly to be rejected. The Fathers were wise but not infallible. But even less infallible is the reason of men less wise. In his epilogue Erigena recognizes the imperfection and fallibility of his doctrine, and submits it, to be accepted or rejected, to the reader's own judgment, which must remain for the reader the ultimate norm of truth. *Let each abound in his own sense,* until the light of perfect vision shall come in the life beyond.[5]

The subordination of authority to reason must not be understood to apply to the sacred scripture. This is infallible, being the very word of truth. Nothing should be said about God which is not said there. But the Bible is written in an allegorical style, condescending to our weakness.[6] It must not be understood literally. It must be interpreted, and it is by reason and authority that we interpret it. The Bible is not itself philosophy or authority but the material for them. Philosophy is the interpretation of the Bible. *Religion* and *philosophy* are two names for the same thing, which is the humble worship and rational investigation of the first cause of all things.[7] Faith is "a certain beginning by which knowledge of the Creator begins to be produced in the rational nature";[8] but Erigena knows nothing of a faith which is opposed to reason or which is necessary in addition to reason.

The whole power of discovering the truth of things, he says, is founded on reason and authority;[9] and by these two means he undertakes to investigate nature. The authorities on whom he relies the most frequently are Gregory of Nazianze, Dionysius, and Augustine, whom he considers the most profound interpreters of scripture. He studied Gregory of Nazianze (whom he confused with Gregory of Nyssa) through the writings of his commentator Maximus. His sources include pagan philosophers as well as Christian Fathers; he defends himself against the reproach that he, a

Christian, uses pagan materials by the precedent of the children of Israel despoiling the Egyptians.[10] In this spirit, seizing all that is best wherever it may be found, he constructs his system of metaphysics, which is set forth in the *Division of Nature.* The following three sections are a summary of that system.

## THE LAW OF NATURE

Nature includes all things which are and, in a certain sense, also those which are not. For there are two meanings of non-being. That which is merely the absence of something positive is nothing at all and is not included in nature—for example, *blindness,* which is merely the absence of sight. But another meaning of non-being follows from the definition of being. Objects which are perceptible by the senses or conceivable by the intellect are said to be. Therefore, objects which by the excellence of their nature surpass both the senses and the intellect are said not to be—for example, the *essences* of things, which are neither perceptible nor conceivable. Such objects, strictly speaking, are not—not because they are less than being but because they are more than being. Thus all nature can be divided into that which is and that which is not.[11] But this division based on the concept of being is ambiguous, because being and non-being, in the sense of knowability and transcendence, are relative to the mind which knows or is transcended. A thing *is* insofar as it is known by itself or by some intellect superior to itself, but *is not* insofar as it is unknown by all things inferior to itself, for the inferior cannot comprehend the superior.[12] This ambiguity is aggravated by the various ways in which the word *being* is used: the philosophers say that only eternal things really are; the theologians say that man in the state of sin really is not, because he has abandoned the image of God which is his substance; in the ordinary use of language things which have not yet come into existence are said not to be.[13] A less ambiguous division of nature is provided by the concept of creation. To divide all nature into creator and creature would be insufficient, because a thing may also be both or neither. An exhaustive division distinguishes four species of nature: nature which creates and is not created, nature which is created and creates, nature which is created and does not create, and nature which neither creates nor is created.[14]

We comprehend nature by reason because nature is itself rational. For Erigena as for Plotinus, logic not merely discovers but generates the world. Insofar as we think rationally, our thought reproduces the process by which the world is formed.[15] Dialectic is the art of disputing; it is also the process of nature.

Dialectic includes two processes, division and analytic. Division differentiates essence into its genera, genera into their species, species into their individuals, and individuals into their parts. Analytic resolves parts into their wholes, wholes into their species, species into their genera, and genera into their essence. The two processes are correlative; they give the same information and describe the same facts, but from opposite points of view. The beginning of the one is the end of the other. *All things are resolved into the same unity from which they are derived;* this is the fundamental law of dialectic and of nature. This law and these two processes, or rather two aspects of one process, are found in all parts of nature and in nature as a whole.[16]

In the visible world this process appears as motion in space and time, and this law appears as the law that motion is cyclical. "The end of all motion is its beginning; for it terminates at no other end save its own beginning from which it begins to be moved and to which it tends ever to return, in order to cease and rest in it." [17] This cyclical law is observed in all cosmic movements and all vital processes.

In the intelligible world this law is the fundamental principle of all the sciences, that is, of the "seven liberal arts." Grammar begins with the letter, from which all writing is derived and into which it is analyzed. Rhetoric begins with a definite question, from which the whole argument is derived and to which it returns. Dialectic begins with essence, from which all forms are developed and into which they are resolved. Arithmetic begins with unity, from which all numbers are developed and into which they are resolved. Geometry begins with the point, from which all figures are developed and into which they are resolved. Music begins with the tone, from which all symphonies are developed and into which they are resolved. Astronomy begins with the moment, from which all motion is developed and into which it is resolved.[18]

Metaphysics, likewise, begins with God, from whom all things are developed and into whom they are resolved. In nature as a whole, division is creation, by which all things emanate, by successive stages, from the divine unity. Analytic is called return, because all things return, through the same stages, to the same unity. All things flow constantly from God as water flows constantly from a spring, and tend ever to return to him as water tends ever to return to its level.[19] God alone is without motion because, being the beginning and end of all things, he has himself neither beginning nor end.[20] The flux of all things is not a motion in time, because all time is comprehended within one part of the process.[21] It is not a cycle which repeats itself, but an eternal cycle, and the two aspects of the process are simultaneously eternal; nature is eternal, but not static. It is eternally dynamic, moving by the dialectical process of division and return.

## THE DIVISION OF NATURE

### *God*

The unity from which all division begins is called God (*Deus*, Θεός), which means *seer* or *runner,* because it sees (θεωρῶ) all things and runs (θέω) into all things.[22] We do not know what God is, not because of any weakness of our intellect but because he is infinite and therefore objectively unknowable.[23] God himself does not know what he is, because he is not anything,[24] not being included in any of the ten categories of being.[25] Therefore, nothing can be predicated of God literally and affirmatively. All that is said of him is said either figuratively or negatively. Affirmative theology affirms all positive things of God, but in a figurative sense, meaning that he is the cause of all things which are. For example, we say, "God is good," but this means only that he is the cause of all good things. Negative theology denies all things of God, and its statements are literally true. We say, "God is not good," not because he is bad but because he transcends goodness. Literally, God is not even God, because he transcends seeing and running; God is not, because he transcends being. The two kinds of theology can be combined by inventing words which will make both statements simultaneously. These words are formed with the prefix *super,* meaning *more than.* Thus, we say, "God is supergood." This means: God is not good himself, but he is the cause of all good things. Likewise, God is supergoodness; God is super-God; God super-is.[26] The relation between God and all things which are is expressed by Dionysius' phrase, "the superbeing of Divinity is the being of all things." [27]

Although we do not know what God is, we infer from the existence of the world that he is—meaning, not that he is as any intelligible essence, but merely that he exists as the cause of all things.[28] This inference is threefold. We observe that things are, and infer that their cause is. We observe that things form not a random collection but a marvelously arranged world, and infer that their cause is wise. We observe that things are not static but in constant motion, all things being alive, and infer that their cause is life. Thus God, considered not in himself but as the cause of all things, has three aspects: he is, he is wise, and he lives. His being is called the Father, his wisdom is called the Son, his life is called the Holy Ghost—words which denote not the three aspects themselves but their relations to each other.[29] (Thus Erigena demonstrates the existence of the three persons of the Trinity by the cosmological argument, the argument from design, and the argument from motion, respectively.)

God's being is his essence, what he is—to use figuratively a word which applies strictly only to creatures. His wisdom is his power, what he can do. His life is his operation, what he does. Essence, power, and operation (*essentia, virtus, operatio;* οὐσία, δύναμις, ἐνέργεια), in God or in anything, are not three parts which compose the substance but a simple and inseparable unity.[30] None of them has meaning without the others. Neither God nor creature could be without any power or operation, nor have power without being or operation, nor operate without being or power. Although the Son and the Holy Ghost are in a certain sense derived from the Father, so that only the Father is without any source, they are nowise made or created by him, but are coeternal and coessential with him. God, therefore, including all three persons, constitutes nature which creates and is not created.[31]

## Creation

All things created by God are created in the image of God and are therefore trinities consisting of essence, power, and operation. These three are the substance of the thing; all else is accident. As in the Trinity of God, these three are an inseparable unity, but they are distinct aspects of that unity. In a tree, for example, these aspects are for it to be, to be able to grow, and actually to grow.[32] The essence is the unknowable being of the thing; the power is its specific character; the operation is its particular movement. All things subsist in these three ways. Therefore, there is a threefold creation of things: their essence is created by the essence of God; their power is created by the power of God; and their operation is created by the operation of God—that is, by the Father, the Word, and the Holy Ghost, respectively. Thus there are three stages in the division of nature: nature is divided into non-being and being, that is, superessence and essence; essence is divided into genera and their species; species are divided into individuals. These divisions are accomplished, respectively, by the three persons of the Trinity: the Father wills, the Son makes, and the Holy Ghost perfects.[33]

The Father wills. That is, God, in his infinite goodness, eternally wills, sees, knows, and makes all things. For him, willing, seeing, knowing, and making are the same. They are the creative act by which all things pass from non-being to being. This act of God is his essence; the creation of the universe is not in God by accident, but by a certain ineffable law that effects subsist eternally in their cause.[34] God does not know things because they are; they are because he knows them, and his knowledge of them is their essence.[35] The essence of things is simple and for us unknowable. We cannot know what things are, but can only know that they are and facts about them. Four attributes common to all things follow from the fact of their creation by God: all things are eternal, made, good, and incorruptible.[36] They are eternal because the will by which they are created is eternal; they exist not only throughout all time but outside all time; with regard to time, they are co-eternal with God. This does not prevent their existing in time also. They are made because their being is dependent on and derived from God; with regard to cause, they are not coeternal with God, in the way in which the Son is coeternal with the Father. This does not prevent their being makers also. They are good because God wills nothing bad; consequently there is no evil in nature. This does not prevent their appearing evil to persons who do not consider the whole of which they are parts, like dark spots which contribute to the beauty of a whole picture. They are incorruptible because there is nothing evil to corrupt them. This does not prevent their freely willing irrational and illicit movements.

The Son makes. That is, God, in his infinite wisdom, eternally divides the created essence into the eternal ideas, which are called the primordial causes,[37] because they cause and create all things. These include, for example, goodness, essence, life, reason, intelligence, wisdom, power, beatitude, truth, eternity, greatness, love, peace, unity, perfection.[38] They are the forms of things, not the visible qualitative forms but the intelligible substantial forms, by participation in which all things subsist, that is, have their separate and special properties or powers;[39] a tree is able to grow because it participates in life. These ideas, existing in the mind of God, contain the substances of all things; man, for example, is most correctly defined as "a certain intellectual notion eternally made in the divine mind."[40] Made in the divine wisdom, they are themselves wise, knowing themselves and all things of which they are the principles.[41] They can be considered in two ways: in themselves, and as the causes of their effects.[42] Considered in themselves, they transcend the world, and so are incomprehensible. They are simple, indivisible, inseparable, and equal. They are not related to each other as species to genus. They are remote from their effects; they seek their perfection only in the Word of God; they are the Word of God.[43] But considered as the causes of their effects, they are immanent in the world, and so become knowable. Viewed in their effects, they have an order among themselves. When the class of things participating in one cause is included in the class of those participating in another, the former cause is called a species of the latter. All things are good, therefore goodness is the summum genus; some good things are, therefore essence is a species of goodness; some things which are are animate, therefore life is a species of essence; some animate things are rational, therefore reason is a species of life.[44] Thus the primordial causes are both transcendent and immanent. "The principal causes both come forth into those things of which they are the causes and do not abandon the principle, that is the wisdom of the Father, in which they are made; while remaining invisible in themselves, ever hidden by the obscurity of their excellence, they do not cease to appear, brought forth in their effects as into a certain light of knowledge."[45] Considered in their relation to the Word, the primordial causes are created; considered in their relation to their effects, they create; they constitute, therefore, nature created and creating.[46]

The Holy Ghost perfects. That is, God, in his infinite activity, leads forth the primordial causes into their effects, dividing the eternal ideas into the particular things, both intelligible and visible, which participate in them.[47] These intelligible and visible things are the theophanies or manifestations by the being, order, and motion of which God is known to be, to be wise, and to be life. They are not different things from the primordial causes but a different aspect of the same things. The effects are related to the causes as words are related to the voice which speaks them; they are subsequent not in time but in order of causality. Unlike the eternal causes, they form genera and species, they come into being through generation, they move in time and space, and they are subject to accidents. They include all essences (which in this aspect are more properly called *natures*),[48] all qualities, all quantities, and all things comprised in the other categories. Separately, that is, apart from their combinations, they are incorporeal, incorruptible, and invisible. A combination of a certain quality and a certain quantity produces matter, which is not a new thing but merely a result of the combination—just as the combination of light and an opaque body produces a shadow, without in any way affecting either the light itself or the body itself.[49] Matter itself, apart from the forms it receives, is likewise invisible and even indefinable. Like a shadow, it is almost nothing at all. It is merely a formlessness or mutability capable of receiving forms. Nevertheless, not being a mere lack or absolute nothing, it is a part of nature. When, at a certain time, matter is joined to a certain form (not a substantial form but a visible form or shape), a visible body is produced.[50] Thus bodies are composed of incorporeal things: qualities, quantities, forms, and times. They are not substances, being composed only of accidents, and are therefore corruptible, for they can be resolved into the accidents which compose them; when these are taken away, nothing remains. All these accidents are accidents of an essence and substantial form, but not of the body; rather, the body is an accident of the accidents. In every body, therefore, three aspects are considered: the matter, that is, quality and quantity, of which it is made; the qualitative form which makes it a solid and visible body; and the eternal essence or substantial form of which these are the accidents.[51] All the particular effects of the primordial causes, including the matter and bodies produced by their combinations, participate in the primordial causes, but nothing participates in them; they may make other things by combining preexisting elements, but they do not create anything by emanation from themselves. They constitute, therefore, nature created and not creating.[52]

The substance of every creature is threefold: it is the essence of the thing, that is, God's knowledge of it, by which it is made to be; it is the eternal form of the thing, established among the primordial causes in the Word, by which it is defined to be what it is; and it is the particular thing, moving in time and subject to accidents, by which it is manifested. (The last aspect of the substance must not be confused with its accidents or with its material body.) Thus all things are both eternal and temporal.

All things always were, in the Word of God, causally, in force and potency, beyond all places and times, beyond all generation made in place and time, beyond all form and species known by sense and understanding, beyond all quality and quantity and other accidents by which the substance of any creature is understood to be, but not what it is. But also, all things were not always, for before they flowed forth by generation into forms and species, places and times, and into all the accidents which happen to their eternal substance immutably established in the Word of God, they were not in generation, they were not in space, nor in time, nor in the proper forms and species to which accidents happen. [53]

The Father creates in the Word the primordial causes of all things, and these perfect the world by their procession through generation into the plurality of things, from the beginning of the world to the end when it shall cease to be.[54]

## Note on Erigena's Doctrine of Creation

An examination of Erigena's doctrine of creation will show to what extent he should be called a pantheist. We may define relative monotheism as the doctrine that God is the necessary cause of all things; he makes them from preexisting matter; this is the position of Plato. Absolute monotheism is the doctrine that God is also the sufficient cause of all things; he creates them from nothing; this is the position of Augustine. Emanationism is the doctrine that God is also the source of all things; he generates them from his own substance; this is the position of Plotinus. Pantheism is the doctrine that God also is all things; he is the only thing which exists; this is the position of Spinoza. In relative monotheism God is the maker and things are his products. In absolute monotheism God is the creator and things are his creatures. In emanationism God is the source and things are his emanations. In pantheism God is the reality and things are his appearances. We will enquire first whether Erigena is a relative monotheist; if he is, whether he is also an absolute monotheist; if he is, whether he is also an emanationist; if he is, whether he is also a pantheist.

That he is a relative monotheist is shown by his doctrine that God is the first cause of all things.[55]

That he is also an absolute monotheist is shown by his explicit statement that both the forms according to which things are made and the unformed matter of which material things are made are themselves creatures of God.[56]

That he is also an emanationist is shown by his explanation of the phrase *creation from nothing*. The *nothing* from which the world is created is not the absolute nothing which is a mere absence of something; if so, the thing of which it is the absence must have preexisted in order to become absent—which is absurd.[57] The *nothing* from which the world is created is that nothing or non-being which is so called because, transcending all categories and surpassing all comprehension, it is above all being—that is, it is God.[58]

That he is also a pantheist is shown by his doctrine that God is the only reality; other things which are said to be are theophanies or appearances of God; in him all things are one. Things exist only insofar as they are willed and seen by God, but he wills and sees nothing other than himself, because a simple nature does not include within itself anything which is not itself; therefore all things are God and God is all things.[59] "God sees nothing except himself, because there is nothing outside himself, and everything which is in him is himself."[60] The Word of God is the unity of all things because it is all things, and it is the plurality of all things because its diffusion is the subsistence of all things. Nothing outside God is essential, because all things are nothing else but participations of him who alone subsists; therefore Creator and creature are one.[61]

Erigena does not say that there is only one substance. He says that there are many substances, and that even the accidents of substances may become in turn the substances of other accidents. Even in the return of all things to God they preserve their separate substances. But it must be remembered that Erigena thinks in the terms of Greek theology, according to which God is one essence in three substances; consequently, the words *essence* and *coessential* in Erigena mean the same as the words *substance* and *consubstantial* in other Latin theologians. If he is not a pantheist, because God and creature have two substances; then he is not even a monotheist, because Father and Son have two substances. If he is a monotheist because Father and Son have one essence, then he is also a pantheist because God and creature have one essence. He speaks of the "essences of things" in the plural; but these "essences" are unknowable and indiscernible, and always contrasted with the powers and operations by which things are distinguished from each other. God and creature are not coessential in the full sense in which Father and Son are coessential—that would not be pantheism, for it would imply the equality of God and creature. But God and creature are coessential in the sense that they have only one essence and that essence is God.[62] "The superbeing of Divinity is the being of all things."

It may be objected that Erigena's philosophy involves the concept of creation, and that if there is creation the creature is other than the creator. Erigena's solution of this difficulty is explicit and uncompromising. In the process of creation God is not only the creator but also the creature; when he creates, he creates himself and nothing but himself. The making of all beings is God's manifestation of himself, which is his creation of himself.[63]

God himself is the maker of all things and is made in all things; when he is sought above all things, he is not found in any essence, for he is not yet being; but when he is understood in all things, nothing subsists in them save him alone. Nor is he one thing and not another thing, but he is all things. First, descending from the superessentiality of his nature, in which he is said not to be, he is created by himself in the primordial causes, and is made the source of all essence, of all life, of all intelligence, and of all which gnostic contemplation considers in the primordial causes. Then, descending from the primordial causes (which occupy a certain middle ground between God and creature, that is, between that ineffable superessentiality beyond all understanding and the substantially manifested nature visible to pure souls), he is made in their effects and appears manifestly in his theophanies. Then he proceeds through the manifold forms of the effects, even to the last order of all nature, in which bodies are comprised. And thus, coming forth successively into all things, he makes all things, and is made all things in all things, and returns into himself, recalling all things into himself, and while he is made in all things he does not cease to be above all things.[64]

## The Fall of Man

Among the creatures existing both eternally as a primordial cause and temporally as the particular effects of that cause is man. Man consists of soul and body.[65] The essence of the soul is the intellect, the power of the soul is the reason, and the operation of the soul is the inner sense; these form a coessential unity in three substantially distinct motions. The intellect or spirit is that supreme immutable motion of the soul which is directed in contemplation toward God; this mystical contemplation, like God its object, is unknowable, and so man cannot know his own essence. The reason, which is born of the intellect, defines the unknowable God as the cause of all things and investigates all things as they exist eternally in the primordial causes; this is wisdom or theology. The inner sense, which proceeds from the intellect through the reason, discerns and distinguishes the images of particular things received from the outer sense, dividing and analyzing them according to the law of dialectic; this is science or physics.[66] The body also has three aspects. First, there is the fivefold outer sense, a certain union of soul and body, by which the physiological images formed in the sense organs by external stimuli are transformed into mental images; it is by the outer sense that falsity enters the soul. Secondly, there is the life or vital motion by which the soul animates, nourishes, augments, unifies, rules, and moves the body. Finally, there is the body itself, that is, the immortal and immutable spiritual body or form created coeternally with the soul as a consubstantial part of human nature, not the mortal material body, which is not part of human nature but an instrument or garment added to man as a result of sin.[67]

Man is the unity of all creatures. He is intellect, reason, sense, life, and body—and there is no other nature besides these except God. As intellect he is equal to the angels, than which nothing (that is, God) is higher; as material body he is equal to inanimate matter, than which nothing (that is, a mere lack of any being) is lower; as life and as sense he is equal to the plants and to the animals, which are intermediate in dignity.[68] But furthermore, all creatures are made in man, that is, have their place in man. The place of a thing is not the body which surrounds it, because bodies are comprised in the category of quantity, which is generically distinct from the category of place. The place of a thing is its boundary or limit, that is, its definition. All definitions are included in the sciences, which are in the mind; therefore all places are in the mind.[69] A thing is made only in the mind which defines and understands it. All things are made in the divine mind, but they may be made in other minds also. "You and I, when we argue, are made in each other. For when I understand what you understand, I become your understanding and am made in you, in a certain ineffable way."[70] Man defines and understands all things, intelligible or sensible, which are, and so all things are made in man. Just as God's knowledge of things is their essence, so man's knowledge of the same things is also their essence. The knowledge of creative wisdom, the Word of God, which sees all things made in it by the Father before they are made, is the first and causal essence of all creatures and the ground of all that is understood about that essence; and the cognition of created wisdom, human nature, which likewise knows all things made in it by the Word before they are made, is the second and effective essence of all creatures, an effect of the former, and the subject of all the accidents which are discerned about this essence. Not that a thing has two essences, but we consider the same essence either as subsisting in the eternal causes or as understood in their effects; in the former case it surpasses all understanding, while in the latter case it is understood from its accidents to be, although in neither case can we know what it is.[71] Since that which understands is prior in dignity to that which is understood, man is the first creature, and all other creatures are created in him.

Man is created as the eternal idea of humanity, without division into sexes or multiplication into individual men. Humanity is created in paradise, that is, in the integrity of human nature, soul and spiritual body, capable of beatitude.[72] It has a free choice between two kinds of knowledge, allegorically represented in the book of Genesis by the two trees of paradise. *Of every tree of paradise thou shalt eat, but of the tree of the knowledge of good and evil thou shalt not eat.* The *every-tree* (or *tree of life*) is the Word of God, in which every thing exists eternally. The *mixed-knowledge-tree* is the nature of visible things, which offer good knowledge to those who understand them spiritually in their reasons, but fatal knowledge to those who desire them carnally contrary to the divine command. From the moment of its creation, before proceeding into individual men, humanity (called *Adam*) eternally chooses the fatal knowledge of visible things, seduced by its outer sense (called *Eve*), which is dominated by an illicit and carnal delight in these things (called *the serpent*). In choosing this knowledge it abandons the contemplative knowledge of the Word of God of which it is also capable.[73] This choice is irrational and illicit but not evil. "Who would call evil that which proceeds from the free choice of a rational creature?" [74] The choice, being

free, is without cause, and is not in any sense made by God.[75] It
does not corrupt human nature, which, like all God's creatures,
is incorruptible; [76] but it has certain consequences both for humanity itself and for the whole universe insofar as it is made in
humanity.

The first consequence for humanity is a blessing by God. God
never curses or punishes anything he has made, but always blesses
and helps his creatures.[77] The belief that God curses or punishes
humanity for its fall is a misinterpretation of the book of Genesis.
He curses only the serpent, that is, irrational carnal desire, which
he did not make. He says to the woman: *I will multiply thy sor-*
*rows and thy conceptions; in labor shalt thou bring forth children;*
that is, humanity will arrive at truth, but by the laborious method
of empirical knowledge through the outer sense, instead of by
direct contemplation of the Word of God. *And thou shalt be under*
*thy husband's power, and he shall have dominion over thee;* this,
not a curse but a blessing, is a promise that eventually the outer
sense will be subjected to the intellect and so humanity will be
restored to felicity. The angel with the flaming sword is placed
at the gate of paradise to light the path so that humanity may
find its way back. The second consequence is the creation by humanity, with God's assistance, of its material body, to serve it as
a necessary instrument in the condition into which its choice of
sense knowledge has brought it.[78] The third consequence is the
division of human nature into two sexes and its multiplication by
sexual reproduction. If human nature chose contemplative knowledge in the spiritual body instead of sensual knowledge in the
material body, this division would not be necessary, for it would
multiply at one moment into all the myriads of its individuals, just
as the angelic nature does.[79]

This choice also has a consequence for the universe of all things,
the essence of which is man's knowledge of them. It is that they

exist in him not as intelligible and eternal ideas but only as sensible and temporal individuals, forming material bodies by the union of qualities, quantities, forms, and times. Thus they are separated from their eternal and undivided existence in the primordial causes, and do not return to the original unity in which they are created in the Word of God. Man, by his fall, segregates the corporeal from the spiritual. He divides things without reuniting them, contrary to the law of nature.[80]

## THE RETURN OF NATURE

### The Return of All Creatures to God

All things have a natural motion the end of which is the same as its beginning; they always seek the source from which they are derived; their motion never ceases until they attain this end; in it alone they come to rest.[81] Bodies are resolved into matter, matter into qualities, qualities into causes, causes into God. Compound material bodies are inevitably resolved into the formless elements of which they are composed. Matter, which is nothing but a union of qualities and quantities, is resolved into those qualities and quantities, and so ceases to exist as matter. It is not annihilated, but transformed into the intelligible and more real things of which it is composed. These intelligible things are resolved into the eternal substances of which they are accidents and into the primordial causes of which they are effects. This is accomplished by knowledge; the effects acquire a knowledge of their cause and so become united to the cause in the sense that that which understands becomes one with that which is understood.[82] The particular things are not annihilated but perfected, according to their natural desire. They exist eternally, but in passing into their eternal causes by knowledge of them they cease to exist temporally. Therefore this temporal world will come to an end after a finite duration of time.[83] The primordial causes, turning from the knowledge of their effects to the knowledge of the Word of God, are resolved into the Word, so that, while the substances remain eternal, nothing appears in them except the divinity.[84]

As all things are derived originally from God by various intermediate steps, so all things are resolved ultimately into God by the same intermediate steps. Thus God is the beginning, the middle, and the end of all things—beginning because all things are from him by participation of his essence, middle because all things live and move and have their being in him, end because all things seek their perfection and the end of their motion in him.[85] As beginning he creates, as middle he is created, but as end he neither creates nor is created. When all his creatures return into him and are at rest in him, nothing further emanates from him. Therefore God considered as the end to which all things return constitutes nature which neither creates nor is created.[86]

Diffusion is goodness; reunion is love. God as cause of all things is supreme goodness [87] and as end of all things is supreme love. Love is the end and quiet cessation of the natural motion of all moving things, beyond which no motion continues; it is the connection and bond by which the universe of all things is joined together in an ineffable sympathy and insoluble unity.[88] God as goodness and God as love, the first cause of all things and final end of all things, are the same; the fact that they are identical is the fundamental law of nature.

## The Restoration of Man

The return of all creatures to God is a rational process—but there is an irrational element in the universe. This is not matter (which is part of the rational world created by God) but sin. By sin man remains separated from God, and all creatures remain in man separated from their eternal causes in the Word of God.

In order to restore man and the universe existing in man to their original unity according to their natural desire, God becomes man.[89] Christ, by his resurrection, frees humanity from its material body, undoes the division of human nature into two sexes, restores it to paradise, and reunites it to the essence of God.[90]

Since in the incarnation the Word assumes human nature, and all human beings participate equally in human nature, all human beings without exception are saved in Christ and restored to paradise.[91] The first step in their restoration is the death of the material body. This death is wrongly called a punishment of sin; the creation, not the death, of the material body is a result of sin; its death is the beginning of our restoration and so might better be called the death of death. The body is dissolved into the elements of which it is composed. The gross qualities of its parts are transformed into the light and spiritual qualities of those elements. The various parts do not cease to be related to each other, for, although the sense sees them as separated, the reason understands that they still form a human body. The soul does not cease to exist nor to administer the body, but rules it all the more easily when it is dissolved into the elements, the tenuous nature of which is much more like the spiritual nature of the soul than the gross nature of the material body was. The second step is the general resurrection, when each person will receive his own body again from the elements. The body will have only the tenuous qualities of the elements; that is, it will not be a gross and corruptible material body but the light and incorruptible spiritual body, without sex, which is part of human nature as originally created. The third and final step is the transformation of the spiritual body into the soul and of the whole soul into the intellect which is its essence. The spiritual body is transformed into the vital motion, the vital motion into the sense, the sense into the reason, and the reason into the intellect. These transformations of intelligible substances are like that of water into vapor—the substance remains but the quality and quantity and other accidents change. The inferior nature passes over into the superior, not so as to perish but so as to be perfected in it. By the death of the material body man is freed from the results of his fall; by the resurrection of the spiritual body he is restored to paradise; by the resolution of his whole nature into the intellect he returns to the essential unity from which all divisions of his nature are derived.[92]

Since in the incarnation the Word assumes human nature, and human nature includes all created nature, the Word assumes all created nature, and all creatures without exception are saved in Christ and restored to their primordial causes. The primordial causes are made in the Word of God and the particular effects are made in humanity; consequently causes and effects are united in Christ. God became man in order to save in his humanity the effects of the causes which he possesses eternally in his divinity, and to recall them into their causes, so that they might be saved in them, together with the causes themselves.[93] The general resurrection will be a resurrection not only of man but of all creatures. The visible appearances and masses of bodies will not rise but will return with man and in man into their immediate causes, which are their intelligible natures made in man; for the true nature of the sensible world is intelligible, being a union of incorporeal substances, not an accumulation of corporeal masses. Then the whole human nature, including the natures of all creatures, will return into the primordial causes. *Heaven and earth shall pass away,* and with them everything sensible, spatial, temporal, and mutable.[94] In so doing they will not perish but will on the contrary be saved. If the return of visible things into their invisible causes were prevented, that would be not only contrary to their natural desire but utterly fatal, for all things would degenerate and perish if they did not return to their source; all effects would perish and consequently all causes would perish. The whole of creation, therefore, is saved by the incarnation of the Word of God.[95]

## The Deification of the Elect

All men will return to paradise, but all men will not eat of the tree of life. All men participate equally in human nature and therefore share equally in the restoration of that nature to its original state of eternal life, but men differ in merit and therefore only certain ones are united to God in eternal beatitude. Human nature is restored in all its members but deified only in the elect.[96] Restoration is accomplished by nature cooperating with grace; deification, which exalts man above his nature, by grace alone.[97]

Even in the sinful, who in this life have loved temporal things rather than God, human nature will not be punished. After the resurrection human nature will exist eternally immaculate, in the sinful no less than in the elect. It will be free from all deception when all things have returned into their causes so that only truth appears. It will be free from all vice when all opportunity for vice has been destroyed. But, although God never punishes anything which he has made, he does permit to be punished, in that which he has made, that which he has not made.[98] That is, he permits to be unsatisfied, in human nature, its perverse will. Human nature, made by God, is eternally good and never sins. The perverse will sins and is punished; but the perverse will is not a natural accident or motion of human nature but an abuse of man's free choice moving irrationally in opposition to his rational nature; being nothing but a lack of natural will, it is not created by God but is without cause and outside nature. The perverse will endures with the images of the temporal things which it desires, but its desire must ever be unsatisfied when all temporal things have ceased to exist. Finding only the unsubstantial images of the things it loves, it will be tortured with a perpetual flame of unfulfilled desire.

This is the torment of the damned. But no men are damned or tormented—only their perverse will; the men themselves are restored and perfected when their perverse will can no longer rule them.

The elect are those upon whom God has bestowed not only the gifts of nature but also the donations of grace by which they merit to transcend human nature and be deified by a superintellectual knowledge and love of God. This knowledge and this love have their roots in the science and the action of this life—a science which proceeds from knowledge of self to knowledge of the theophanies created by God in human nature, and an action which spurns and destroys the flesh and all things perceived by sense in order to renew the spirit. After the resurrection, when the whole man has been transformed into the spirit, the spirit will be absorbed by a knowledge of all creation and faith will be replaced by vision. Then, science will be absorbed by wisdom, that is, direct contemplation of truth in the primordial causes and in God—but always in his theophanies, never in his essence, which is absolutely unknowable. Finally, the purest souls will be transformed into God by that pure contemplation which makes the subject disappear in its object.[99] Thus human nature, and with it and in it all nature, is perfected, returning to its source.

Just as the air appears to be all light, and the molten iron to be all fiery—nay fire itself, their substances nevertheless remaining; so it is understood by the intellect that after the end of this world every nature, whether corporeal or incorporeal, will seem to be only God, the integrity of the nature remaining, so that God, who is in himself incomprehensible, will be somehow comprehended in the creature, and the creature will by an ineffable miracle be turned into God.[100]

## ERIGENA'S PLACE IN HISTORY

The *Division of Nature,* condemned as heretical in 1225, was little studied in the later Middle Ages and had little influence on the development of philosophy, at least among the more orthodox and famous writers. It marks the end of an epoch; Erigena was not so much the first medieval as the last ancient philosopher. There is a continuity in the movement which includes the Greek philosophers and the Christian Fathers from Plato to Erigena. The real medieval philosophy begins in the eleventh century with Anselm of Canterbury. Ancient philosophy was the search for truth. Medieval philosophy no longer searched for truth, for it already possessed truth in the dogma of the Church; it was the attempt to understand that truth and explain how it is known. Truth was the object, not the presupposition, of ancient philosophy, which was the attempt to learn the truth about nature by means of the Greek logic and the Christian revelation. Erigena's doctrine was the last formulation of that ancient wisdom.

His system has two central concepts—eternal divinity as the unity of the universe of causes, and eternal humanity as the unity of the universe of effects. Separated in Adam, they are reunited in Christ. God comprehends all things as their essence, and man comprehends all things by knowledge. But just as it is human nature, rather than individual men, which falls and is restored, so it is human nature which knows. Ancient philosophy began in Plato with the affirmation that the object of knowledge is eternal, and it ended in Erigena with the affirmation that the subject of knowledge is also eternal.

# Chapter II. ANSELM OF CANTERBURY

## THE PROBLEM OF KNOWLEDGE

KNOWLEDGE has been the center of interest for philosophers since the eleventh century. For medieval philosophers the truth about the being of nature was given by Christianity, just as for modern philosophers it is given by science. The central problem was, how we know this truth, and the most fundamental question was, whether we can understand it by our own reason or must believe it by faith in revelation. A controversy over this question heralded the dawn of medieval philosophy in the eleventh century.

A leading champion of reason was Berengar of Tours, professor of the monastic school of St. Martin at Tours. Repeatedly condemned for his heresies by Church councils, he remained unconverted, because he rejected the authority of the established Church. Following Erigena, he admitted the truth of the scriptures but insisted on the necessity of interpreting them rationally. Not by decrees of the Church, the moral corruption of which has destroyed its authority, but by reason, which is the image of God in man, do we attain truth. Reason arrives at truth by dialectic, which is superior to all authorities and which was used by Augustine and even by Christ himself. Whatever is illogical, notably the doctrine of transubstantiation, is necessarily false.

The opposite extreme was represented by Peter Damian, prior of the hermitage of Fonte-Avellana in Italy, which was celebrated as a center of excessive asceticism. His caustic pen attacked body and mind alike, condemning both carnal and intellectual indulgences. From the omnipotence of God he inferred such consequences as that the past, as well as the future, is contingent, depending on God's will. If this seems irrational, the fault is with our reason, or rather with our grammar, which is not adapted to the discussion of eternal things. Human wisdom, when treating the scriptures, must not arrogate authority to itself, but, like the handmaid of a noble lady, follow obsequiously, lest it go astray and lose the way of truth by following a verbal argument.

Lanfranc, the Italian prior of the Benedictine abbey of Bec in Normandy, afterward archbishop of Canterbury, defended the priority of faith without denying the validity of reason. In a book against Berengar he insisted that the authority of the Fathers and of the Church must be followed in theological questions, which transcend the power of reason. But dialectic is useful for interpreting the scripture and for confirming its teachings.

## ANSELM OF CANTERBURY

Lanfranc's disciple Anselm undertook to solve this question by demonstrating that reason and faith lead to the same conclusions.

Anselm of Canterbury was born at Aosta in Piedmont in 1033. He left his native land at the age of twenty-four, and, after traveling three years in France and studying under Lanfranc at Bec, he became a Benedictine monk. At first he hesitated to enter the abbey of Bec for fear his own learning would shine less brilliantly beside Lanfranc's, but finally overcame that unmonkish scruple. His humility was rewarded when Lanfranc left Bec three years later and Anselm was made prior, which was practically equivalent to being abbot, the abbot being an old man unable to manage the monastery's affairs personally. When the old abbot died fifteen years later, Anselm became abbot, and held that position another fifteen years. At Bec he became famous for his piety, his miracles, and his theological teaching. He devoted a great deal of time to pious exhortations, in which, according to his admiring biographer, Anselm, remaining himself indefatigable, invariably exhausted even the hardiest listeners. The last years of his life were less happy. Elected archbishop of Canterbury, Anselm, a good Catholic, was dismayed to find that the English Church, of which he had become primate, did not acknowledge the supremacy of the pope. Twice he went into exile for three years. A reconciliation was finally effected, however, and he died at Canterbury in 1109.

Besides letters, prayers, meditations, and sermons, Anselm wrote several books on theology. Some of these books are dialogues; all are short, and in a clear and orderly style. In them he sets forth the truths of Christianity, not by the authority of the Bible or of the Fathers, but by strictly rational arguments. "Absolutely nothing is to be urged in this work on the authority of Scripture, but the necessity of reason shall briefly prove and the clarity of truth shall clearly show to be true, in plain style and common arguments and simple discourse, whatever the conclusion of the various investigations asserts." [1] Thus he shows his readers that reason and faith lead to the same conclusions—"not in order that they should come through reason to faith, but in order that they should delight in the understanding and contemplation of those things which they believe." [2] The reader who expects mathematically cogent proofs, however, will be disappointed. The reasoning follows rather a sort of moral necessity; that divine justice will vindicate itself is a fundamental premise. The arguments are largely taken from Augustine's works, but are set forth more systematically than by him. Anselm follows Augustine's attitude of *faith seeking understanding*. He begins with faith. He does not try to discover theological truth by reason, for it is given by faith. He tries to understand it by reason, so that belief may become unnecessary. A Christian, he says, ought not to argue why that which the Catholic Church believes, is not; but ever holding that faith indubitably and loving it and living according to it, ought to seek humbly the reason why it is.[3]

In *De fide Trinitatis* he shows that only one person of the Trinity was incarnate because God assumed man in unity of person, not of nature. In *De processione Spiritus Sancti* he shows that the Holy Ghost proceeds from the Son as well as from the Father because it proceeds from the Father by reason of his deity, not his paternity. In *De casu diaboli* he shows that the absence of justice which has been received and then abandoned is a mere negation and therefore not made by God, but is evil and therefore justly punished. In *De conceptu virginali* he shows that Christ, although of the race of Adam, was sinless, because conceived of a virgin, original sin being transmitted only by natural propagation. In *De veritate* he defines truth as rectitude perceptible by the mind alone. In *De voluntate* he distinguishes three meanings of *will:* the instrument of willing, the affection of this instrument, and the use of this instrument. In *De libero arbitrio* he shows that man is always slave in that he cannot attain rectitude of will if he does not have it, and always free in that he cannot be deprived of it if he does have it. In *De concordia* he shows that free choice is consistent with God's prescience, God's predestination, and God's grace. In *De grammatico* he distinguishes between the connotation and the denotation of words—*grammaticus* connotes a quality but denotes a man.

His most important works, however, are the *Monologion,* the *Proslogion,* and the *Cur Deus homo.*

## THE "MONOLOGION"

In the *Monologion,* his longest book, Anselm demonstrates, by reason alone, the principal doctrines of Christianity, and first of all its fundamental doctrine, the existence of God.

All men seek to enjoy those things which they consider good.

Since good things, when compared with each other, are more or less good, there must be an absolute good by which they are judged and which exists in them all. Since all good things are good through it, it alone is good through itself, and so it is the greatest good. Therefore there is one thing supremely good. Similarly, there is one thing supremely great. Only the supremely good can be supremely great; therefore there is something which is the greatest and best of all things which are.

Another proof: Everything which is, is either through something or through nothing. Nothing can be through nothing. Therefore everything is through something. This something is either one or many. If many, then these many are either all through some one thing or else each through itself or else through each other. If they are all through some one thing, then all things ultimately are through that one thing. If each is through itself, then there is some power of existence through self by which they have their existence through self, in which case they are through that power by which they have their existence, and so all things ultimately are through that one power. If they are through each other, then one is through that to which it itself gives being—which is absurd. Therefore there is one thing through which all things which are are. It alone is through itself, and therefore the greatest of all things which are.

A third proof: The natures of things are unequal in dignity; men are better than animals, and animals are better than plants. There must be some nature than which none is better, otherwise there would be an infinity of natures. There is either one such supreme nature or many equally supreme. If many, they are equally so great through some one thing, which is either themselves or something else. If it is themselves, that is, their essence, then they have the same essence and are not many natures but one. If it is something else, then they are less than that through which they are great. Therefore there is one nature superior to all others.

There is therefore one supreme nature, existing through itself, supremely great and good, through which all things have their being, and through which all good things are good.

The supreme nature is through itself, not in the sense of being *made* by or of or through itself, but in the same way in which a light shines through and of itself. All other things are made *by* it. They are made *of* nothing, that is, there is not anything of which they are made. They existed in the reason of their maker before they were made. Their preexistence in this reason is a certain speaking of them—just as an artisan about to make some work of art first says it within himself by a mental conception. Since the supreme substance makes everything only through itself, and since it makes everything through its inner speech, it follows that this inner speech of the supreme essence is the supreme essence.

Just as all things which are are through one thing, so all things which endure endure through one thing. Consequently, where it is not, nothing is. Therefore it is everywhere.

Since the supreme nature is better than any other nature, whatever is absolutely better than its contradictory can be attributed to it. It is living, wise, omnipotent, true, just, blessed, eternal. Whatever is just is just through justice; the supreme essence is just (or anything else) only through itself; therefore the supreme essence is justice. A man can have justice but cannot be justice. The supreme nature does not have justice but is justice. To call it just (or anything else) is to say what it is, not how it is. The supreme nature is many goods, but it is not composite, because a composite is dependent for its existence on the things of which is is composed. Therefore all the goods which the supreme nature is, are one.

The supreme nature, being truth, has neither beginning nor

end; otherwise it would be true before its beginning that there was no truth, and true after its end that there is no truth—which is self-contradictory. It is everywhere and always, although it is not *in* any place or time, because it is not contained in any place or time.

The supreme nature, being immutable, has relations but no accidents, and so is not a substance. It is neither universal nor particular. We call it substance because it exists, and spirit because spirit is the highest essence we know. It alone is absolutely. All other things are not absolutely; but they are not absolutely not, because they are made something by that which alone absolutely is.

Since the supreme Spirit is simple, and since his speaking is himself, his speaking is simple, and so does not consist of many words but is one Word. Since it is not a word describing things already made, but is the preexisting Word according to which things are made, it is not more or less true according as it resembles the things, but all things exist more or less truly according as they resemble it. The supreme Spirit, understanding himself eternally, says himself eternally, and this is his Word, existing coeternally with him whether or not any other essence exists. Derived from the supreme Spirit as an offspring perfectly resembling its parent, the Word is truly begotten.

In the supreme Spirit as in man, understanding is born of memory. Memory and understanding of anything are useless unless that thing is loved or rejected. Therefore, since the supreme Spirit is mindful of and understands himself, he loves himself, and his love proceeds from his memory and understanding, that is, from Father and Son. The supreme Spirit's self-love, being equal to his self-memory and self-understanding, is equal to himself and so is himself. It would exist even if nothing except him existed, and so is itself the supreme essence. It is not made or begotten, but exhaled, by Father and Son, and so is called their Spirit.

The supreme essence is ineffable. All that has been proved about it is to be understood figuratively, not literally.

The supreme essence is unknowable, but an approach to knowledge of it is made by knowledge of that which resembles it. The rational mind resembles it the most closely of all creatures. The more zealously the rational mind concentrates on knowing itself, the more effectively it ascends to the knowledge of the supreme essence; and the more it neglects to know itself, the more it descends from the vision of it.

The rational mind, mindful of and understanding and loving itself, is an image of the supreme essence. It is rational in order to distinguish good and evil, loving the good and rejecting the evil. It is therefore made in order to love the supreme good above all things. But it cannot love it unless it is mindful of it and strives to understand it. Therefore the rational creature ought to devote itself wholly to being mindful of, understanding, and loving the supreme good. It is for this that it has its being. It is made to love the supreme essence endlessly, and therefore it is made to live forever if it forever wills to do that for which it is made. This endless life will be free from all danger and so blessed. The supreme nature, being just, rewards whoever loves it with the object of his desire. Therefore every rational soul which loves the supreme blessedness will eventually possess it. Since obviously it will not abandon its blessedness, it will possess it forever and be forever blessed.

One cannot love that which he does not believe in. Therefore it is necessary to believe in the Trinity. A faith accompanied by love will be a living faith, that is, manifested by good works. The supreme essence in which we believe, since it above all things is to be venerated and prayed to, is called God.

## THE "PROSLOGION"

If the demonstrations of the *Monologion* seem sometimes to lack strict mathematical cogency, nobody was more acutely aware of that fact than Anselm himself. For a long time he sought to discover one clear, flawless, and sufficient proof that God exists and is the supreme good. He finally succeeded, and published his demonstration in the *Proslogion; or, Faith Seeking Understanding*. He begins with a prayer for understanding. "I do not seek to understand in order that I may believe, but I believe in order that I may understand." [4] He then proceeds to the deduction of God's existence, as follows:

Therefore, O Lord, who givest understanding to faith, give to me that, so far as thou knowest to be expedient, I may understand that thou art, as we believe, and art that which we believe. For we believe that thou art something than which nothing greater can be thought. Is there then no such nature, because *the fool hath said in his heart: There is no God?* But surely the very same fool, when he hears this which I say, "something than which nothing greater can be thought," understands what he hears; and what he understands is in his understanding, even if he does not understand that it is. For it is one thing for a thing to be in the understanding; another, to understand that the thing is. For when a painter thinks in advance that which he is about to make, he has indeed in the understanding, but does not yet understand to be, that which he has not yet made. But when he has finally painted it, he both has in the understanding, and understands to be, that which he has finally made. Even the fool therefore is convinced that there is at least in the understanding something than which nothing greater can be thought; because when he hears this he understands it, and whatever is understood is in the understanding. And surely that than which nothing greater can be thought cannot be in the understanding alone. For if it is at least in the understanding, it can be thought to be also in reality—which is greater. If therefore that than which a greater cannot be thought is in the understanding alone, that very thing than which a greater cannot be thought is that than which a greater can be thought—but surely this cannot be. Therefore there exists beyond doubt something than which a greater cannot be thought, both in the understanding and in reality.[5]

The rest of the book shows how not only the existence, but all that is believed concerning the essence, of God is implied by his definition as that than which nothing greater can be thought.

By this argument Anselm believed that he had definitely demonstrated monotheism and refuted *the fool* who *hath said in his heart: There is no God*. The fool found a champion, however, in another Benedictine, Gaunilon, a monk of the abbey of Marmoutier near Tours, who wrote a *Liber pro insipiente* pointing out the fallacies of the *Proslogion*. Gaunilon did not deny that God exists, but he denied that Anselm had proved it. In the first place, he said, the argument that God cannot be thought without his real existence being understood is invalid, because, if so, the thought would not precede the understanding of his real existence, as in the example of the painting. Also, if so, no proof would be necessary. Furthermore, false things which do not exist at all are often thought of and believed to exist. However, the analogy with the painting is false, because the painting, before it is painted, is in the artist's soul, but an external object is distinct from the understanding by which it is conceived. As a matter of fact, we do not have any concept of God, even a false one, because he is not included in any genus known to us; *God* and *something greater than all things* are meaningless words for us. The very fact that God is greater than all things cannot be proved unless it is first proved that he exists. An argument similar to Anselm's could be devised to prove the existence of a most perfect island—which would be absurd. Finally, if I can think myself not to be, when I know with absolute certainty that I am, then I can also think God not to be; if I cannot think myself not to be, then inability to be thought not to be is not peculiar to God.

Anselm replied to this and refuted each of Gaunilon's objections. God is thought by faith before his real existence is understood by reason. Proof of his existence is necessary because he can be thought not to be by one who does not understand what he is. If even unreal things are in thought and understanding, that nowise disproves that God is there also. The example of the painting is only to show that a thing can be in the understanding which is not understood to be, so Gaunilon's distinction between the two cases is irrelevant. God can be known under a genus, because the supreme good is known by the likeness of lesser goods. Anselm does not call God *something greater than all things* but *that than which a greater cannot be thought,* and this phrase can be understood even if what it denotes cannot be understood. The example of the island is irrelevant, for an island is not that than which a greater cannot be thought. All real things are unable to be *understood* not to be—for falsities cannot be understood; but God alone is unable even to be *thought* not to be.

The question raised by Gaunilon, whether Anselm's argument (called "the ontological proof of the existence of God") is sound, has been a point of controversy among philosophers even since. Thomas Aquinas rejects it, saying:

Even if it be granted that everyone understands this name *God* to signify what is said (namely, that than which a greater cannot be thought), it does not follow from this that he understands that which is signified by the name to be in the nature of things, but only in the apprehension of the understanding. Nor can it be argued that it is in reality, unless it be granted that there is in reality something than which a greater cannot be thought—which is not granted by those who maintain that God is not.[6]

Descartes, on the other hand, reasserts it, saying:

It is no less inconsistent to think of a God (that is, a being supremely perfect) to whom existence is lacking (that is, to whom any perfection is lacking) than to think of a mountain to which a valley is lacking.[7]

Kant rejects it, saying:

I simply ask you, whether the proposition, that *this or that thing* . . . *exists,* is an analytical or a synthetical proposition. If the former, then by its existence you add nothing to your thought of the thing. . . . If . . . you admit . . . that every proposition involving existence is synthetical, how can you say that the predicate of existence does not admit of removal without contradiction? [8]

Hegel accepts the validity of the argument but criticizes Anselm's formulation of it, saying:

Undoubtedly God would be imperfect, if he were merely thought and did not also have the determination of Being. But in relation to God we must not take thought as merely subjective; thought here signifies the absolute, pure thought, and thus we must ascribe to him the quality of Being.[9]

## THE "CUR DEUS HOMO"

In *Why God is Man* (*Cur Deus homo*) the same method is extended to the doctrine of the incarnation.

Since rationality is the power of discerning good and evil, man was made rational in order to discern them and consequently to choose the good he discerns and attain the good he chooses. Unless God's purpose in making man is destined to be frustrated, an impossible hypothesis, man must be able to do that for which God made him, that is, attain the good and ultimately the supreme good of celestial beatitude.

Justice, which is essential to the divine order of the universe, requires that sin be either atoned for or punished. To sin is to deprive God of what is owed to him; and every rational creature owes it to God to subject his will to God's will. It is morally intolerable that a creature should not pay, either by recompense or by punishment, for the honor due to God which he has taken away from God. Consequently man, who has sinned against God, depriving God of his due honor by opposing his will, cannot escape his deserved punishment and attain the reward of beatitude unless he makes recompense for his sin. Man alone, however, cannot give due recompense for his sin, because, being now sinful, he cannot restore to God the sinless man he took away from God; and even if he could, just recompense for unjust deprivation requires that more be restored than was taken away. Neither can any other creature give the recompense for him, for in that case man would be justly bound to his redeemer, and so be the latter's slave, instead of being restored to his original state as servant of God and peer of the angels. Furthermore, no creature can be given as recompense, because all creatures are owed to God anyway; nothing less than God is adequate. But God cannot justifiably give himself the recompense for man through mercy, because in that case sinner and non-sinner would be the same before God, justice would be thwarted, and the universe would be disordered. Only man can make satisfaction for his own sin; yet only God is able to make it. Consequently only a person who is both God and man can make the recompense— adequate to make it because he is God, competent to make it because he is man. Such a God-man can exist only if God becomes man.

From the premises that man can attain beatitude and that he cannot do so unless God becomes man, it follows necessarily that God becomes man.

## FAITH AND UNDERSTANDING

Augustine's maxim *believe in order to understand* (*crede ut intelligas*) was adopted by Anselm with a different emphasis. Augustine, brought up as a philosopher, sought as a matter of course to understand; the question was, how? He found the answer to this question when he was converted to Christianity. Do not rely on reason alone but first *believe* in order to understand afterwards. Anselm, brought up as a Christian, believed as a matter of course; the question was, why? He insisted that belief is not enough but is only a first step. Believe not as an end in itself but *in order to understand*. To understand by reason the doctrines which we already believe by faith became an ideal of philosophy, but as the Middle Ages progressed philosophers found this ideal more and more unattainable.

Erigena, as we have seen, relied on reason alone. He sought to understand nature by "reason and authority," but by "authority" he meant the authority of reason, not any non-rational faith either in the Fathers or in the Bible. The Bible may be interpreted, if reason so requires, in a sense the opposite of its superficially apparent meaning. The writings of the Fathers and of the philosophers are authoritative in the way that books on mathematics are authoritative; in them we expect to find truths we would not be able to discover ourselves, but only because the writers are more skillful than we, not because they have any superrational revelation, and any doctrines which are not confirmed by our own reason should not be accepted. If we cannot all agree, *let each abound in his own sense,* concludes Erigena most unCatholicly.

For Anselm faith, which means belief on the authority of revelation, is a source of knowledge independent of reason and coordinate with it. Objectively they are of equal value, since both teach the same truths. But understanding is better, while faith is easier. Faith is given complete and infallible to all believers, while understanding is very difficult to achieve. But as rational beings we seek as our highest good in this life to understand by reason the truths we believe by faith, and the purpose of theology is to replace belief by understanding. If they seem to conflict, we should not, like Berengar, conclude that the faith is in error but should attribute the conflict to the fallibility of reason—not reason as such, but the individual's own reason, which may be incapable of understanding many things. Consequently, Anselm taught that whoever cannot understand any dogma must simply accept it on faith, although he was never forced to that extremity himself.

Abelard, as we shall see, agreed with Anselm that faith and reason teach many of the same truths independently, but with him the emphasis is the opposite. Faith is better, while understanding is easier. Belief is more meritorious than understanding, and nobody who possesses the faith has any need to understand it rationally. Rational understanding is necessary only for those who do not have faith or for theologians who are obliged to defend the rationality of the dogma against the sophistical pseudo-rationalists who deny it. To them Abelard might say, understand in order to believe; but never would he say, believe in order to understand.

For Bernard also faith and reason are independent and equally valid sources of knowledge, but not of the same knowledge. Some of the doctrines of Christianity are understood by reason, and to believe them is unnecessary or rather meaningless. But other essential doctrines are unintelligible for our finite minds. A Christian must believe them; an infidel has no reason to accept them at all. To call understanding a fruit of faith means that mystical vision results from a living faith in Christ, not that the rational understanding of any doctrine replaces belief in that doctrine.

Thomas Aquinas, in the thirteenth century, developed the implications of the distinction between the domain of understanding and the domain of faith by distinguishing the two sciences which are concerned with them. "Philosophy" is the science of that which is known through reason and experience—for example, the existence of God—and it is the same for Christians and infidels. "Theology" is the science which draws conclusions from truths given by revelation—for example, the Trinity of God—and it is possible only for those to whom its premises have been revealed. Theology understands its revealed doctrines in the sense of showing their logical tenability and deducing their consequences but not in the sense of demonstrating the doctrines themselves. Reason alone can accomplish nothing in the science of theology, and an attempt to demonstrate its doctrines only exposes the faith to derision.

Duns Scotus criticized Aquinas for overemphasizing the possibilities of a non-Christian philosophy based on reason alone. The truths knowledge of which are essential for salvation are not logically necessary but contingent on God's will. Therefore they are not known by natural reason but only by revelation. The pagan philosopher ignorant of them inevitably erects a philosophical system in which man's final goal is found in purely natural goods, and he has every reason to suppose that this false philosophy is true. Faith not only supplements but also corrects this philosophy by revealing the supernatural good which is our true goal.

William of Occam, the last great philosopher of the Middle Ages, maintained that we know by reason only that which is immediately obvious or that which can be logically deduced from what is obvious. We know by reason, therefore, only the empirical world of individual things. Even the most elementary truths of Christianity, such as the existence of God, are neither obvious nor demonstrable by rigorous logic; the alleged proofs are fallacious. These truths are known by faith, but they can never be understood by reason.

Thus we see how, while the content of faith remained substantially the same throughout the Middle Ages, its intelligibility varied radically. *Faith seeking understanding (fides quaerens intellectum)* was Anselm's definition of Christian philosophy. As standards of logical rigor became more strict, the domain in which this ideal could be fulfilled became correspondingly smaller. The history of medieval philosophy is the history of the failure and gradual abandonment of faith's search for understanding.

# Chapter III. PETER ABELARD

## THE PROBLEM OF UNIVERSALS

WHEN Plato declared that philosophy is concerned not with particular individuals but with universal ideas, he made the problem of universals a fundamental problem for philosophy. The classical formulation of this problem is given by the third-century Neoplatonist Porphyry, who says at the beginning of his introduction to Aristotle's *Categories:* "Concerning genera and species, whether they subsist or are located only in bare concepts, whether if subsisting they are corporeal or incorporeal, and whether they are separate from sensible things or located in sensible things with respect to which they have their being, I decline to say." This formulation suggests four possible solutions of the problem: (1) that genera and species are incorporeal realities separate from the sensible individuals in which they are manifested; (2) that they are incorporeal realities existing only in the sensible individuals; (3) that they are corporeal realities; and (4) that they are not real but mere concepts in the mind. These possibilities suggest the theories held by the Platonists, Aristotelians, Stoics, and Epicureans, respectively.

Boethius, the sixth-century Christian scholar from whose translations of and commentaries on Aristotle's works the early medieval philosophers learned all they knew of classical logic, was equally noncommittal. In discussing this sentence in Porphyry's *Introduction* he expounded the Aristotelian theory of the species as being the substantial form, that is, an incorporeal reality existing only in sensible individuals, although understood apart from any particular individual by a process of abstraction. But he explained that he did so not because he particularly approved this theory but because the work he was commenting on was an introduction to Aristotle. In his own commentary on the *Categories* Boethius raised the question whether Aristotle was discussing things or words signifying things. This simplified formulation of the problem became the basis of the medieval controversy. The question was very simple: are universals *things* or *words?*

The question was hotly debated by the dialecticians of the French schools at the beginning of the twelfth century. The four principal theories of universals advocated at that time, although not quite the same as those distinguished by Porphyry, were analogous to them and represent the same four philosophical attitudes. They were, respectively, the three *realist* theories—essence theory, indifference theory, class theory—and the *nominalist* theory. In these discussions a certain complication of the problem seems to have resulted from an uncritical acceptance of the rather doubtful assumption that the relation of an individual to its species is similar to that of a species to its genus.

The controversy began with the teaching of Roscelin of Compiegne. According to his theory of nominalism,[1] now known only through the criticism of his opponents, logic is the science of words. Real things are all individuals. Genera and species, universals and particulars, subjects and predicates, even parts of things, are mere logical entities, that is, words, and when logicians discuss these they are talking about words. Universals, therefore, are not real things but words. And words, as defined by Boethius, are in themselves mere breaths of air blown out from the mouth. In themselves, therefore, universals are nothing but breaths of air blown out—a conclusion which led Anselm of Canterbury to remark that logicians holding such opinions should themselves be blown out from discussions of spiritual questions.[2] Roscelin did not hesitate to draw the conclusions which he believed followed from his premises. Since the three persons of the Trinity, although perfectly equal, are three separate things, as is proved by the fact that one was incarnate without the others, the deity which they have in common is a word, not a real thing, and so the three persons could rightly be called three gods. This conclusion led to Roscelin's being condemned for heresy and exiled to England, where his tactless comments on the morals of the English clergy caused him to be reexiled back to France again. The unattractive character which his opponents attribute to him is confirmed by his vulgar invective against Abelard, but his historical importance as one of the founders of medieval philosophy cannot be questioned. To quote Victor Cousin: "He bequeathed to modern philosophy these two great principles: first, that abstractions must not be reified; and second, that the power of the human soul and the secret of its development are largely in language." [3]

*treated as though concrete*

In opposition to this extreme nominalism with its heretical implications, the most distinguished philosopher of the time, William of Champeaux, archdeacon of Paris and professor of dialectic at the cathedral school, taught the extreme realism of the essence theory.[4] His logical works are lost. He is said to have maintained, not only that universals are real things, but that they are the only real things. The same real thing exists essentially, completely, and simultaneously in all the individuals of the species. These individuals have no diversity in their essence but merely variety in their accidents. Any two men differ only through their accidental forms. They have the same material essence, namely, the one human substance, and therefore are essentially the same thing. This essentially one thing is the species man, to which certain forms supervene to make Socrates, others to make Plato; and there is nothing in Socrates which is not identically the same in Plato except these accidents which produce him by informing that matter. A similar relation holds between genus and species; the one genus is the material essence of all its species, which differ from each other only by accidental forms. Thus William upheld the ancient Platonic principle that it is the intelligible idea, not the sensible individual, which is real.

William lectured on dialectic and other subjects at Paris, first at the cathedral school and later at the monastery of St. Victor, which he had founded, and where he continued to teach until he became bishop of Chalons. Most of his students, presumably, silently copied the master's words in their notebooks. But one student, young Abelard, not only insisted on talking in class but made such forceful criticisms of the essence theory that William, with a commendable devotion to truth rather than to his own reputation for infallibility, finally acknowledged that he was convinced. Rejecting his former view as untenable, he proposed a new theory of universals, the so-called indifference theory.[5] Its formula is that the individuals of a species are *the same thing not essentially but indifferently* (that is, by not differing). Two men, to be sure, are one and the same thing. But we must distinguish two meanings of the words *one* and *same*. Things may be one and the same according to *identity of essence* or according to *indifference*. Simon and Peter are one and the same by identity of essence. But Peter and Paul are one and the same by indifference, that is, in being men, in which they do not differ from each other. Strictly speaking, William admits, their common humanity is not the *same* but *similar,* since they are two men. Wherever there are several persons (except in God, whose nature transcends the laws of creatures), there are a corresponding number of substances. The individuals of a species differ, therefore, not only in their forms but in their essences. That in which they are indifferent (not different from each other) is the specific nature, that is, the universal. The universal, therefore, is not the essence of the thing. Nevertheless it is a real thing, not a mere word. Nothing exists which is not an individual. But that which is individual in one respect is species or genus in other respects. Socrates is an individual when considered in the completeness of his sensible nature, because this whole nature is found in nothing else. But if we neglect his peculiar Socratity and consider him only as man, that is, as a mortal rational animal, then he is species, because man can be *predicated of numerically different things with respect to what they are*—which is the definition of species. If we neglect his mortality and rationality and consider him only as animal, with all those attributes, but only those attributes, which being an animal implies, then he is genus. If neglecting all else we consider him only as substance, then he is summum genus. Thus all real things are universals —but by indifference, not by essence. The essence theory is valid only for God, not for universals; God, says William, is in all creatures, or rather creatures are contained in and by him, in such a way that he is always substantially whole and undivided in every particle of things. The indifference theory harmonized the reality of the universal with the integrity of the individual. It enjoyed widespread acceptance, and various modifications of it are found in the doctrines of several teachers of this period.

The class theory is known from an anonymous treatise entitled *Genera and Species*.[6] The author, after criticizing and rejecting the essence, indifference, and nominalist theories, sets forth his own theory of universals and defends it, in typical medieval fashion, both by reasons and by authorities. The species is neither the essence of its individuals, for in that case they would be inseparable; nor the indifferent aspect of its individuals, for in that case the individual would be universal; nor a mere word, for words are nothing at all. In order to avoid the fallacies of the other theories we must understand that the *essence* of a thing is neither first substance (that is, an individual) nor second substance (that is, a universal) but a third nameless sort of substance. The essence of an individual is that which sustains the individual's form, and so it is not the individual as such but only its matter, as contrasted with its form. But it sustains the form of one individual only, and so it is not the species, which is common to all. Every individual is composed of matter and form. Socrates, for example, is composed of *man,* the matter, and *Socratity,* the form. Plato is composed of an indifferent or similar (although not numerically identical) matter and a different form, Platonity. Just as the Socratity which formally constitutes Socrates exists nowhere outside Socrates, so that essence of man which sustains the Socratity in Socrates exists nowhere save in Socrates. A species is the class (*collectio* or *multitudo*) of the essences of the individuals of the same nature. A nature is defined as whatever is of dissimilar creation from all things which are neither it nor of it, whether one essence or many; that is, the essences of all men, together with the class composed of them, constitute a nature, whereas the essences of an arbitrarily selected group of men would not constitute a nature. The species, so defined, is intrinsically a plurality, although denoted by a singular noun. Humanity is not one but many. Not the species as such, but only one part of it, is the essence of the individual; that of man which sustains Socratity does not sustain Platonity. When we call a mass of iron from which a knife and a pen are to be made the matter of the knife and pen, we do not mean that the whole mass is to receive the form of either knife or pen, but that one part is to receive the form of a knife and another part the form of a pen. Likewise when we say that humanity, being predicated of Socrates, inheres in Socrates, we do not mean that all humanity inheres in him, but that a part of humanity inheres in him, the part, namely, which receives the form of Socratity; it is the same figure of speech as saying that I touch a wall when only my finger touches it. Socrates is not *man* but *a man,* and we must avoid the fallacy of univocation involved in identifying the individual with the species. The essence of the individual is of the same nature as the species, but not identical with it, being related to it as member to class. A similar relation holds between species and genus. Each essence which is the matter of an individual consists itself of matter and form. The part of humanity which is the essence of Socrates, for example, consists of *animal,* the matter, and *rationality, mortality, bipedality, etc.,* the substantial forms. The animality which is the essence of the essence of Socrates is indifferent or similar to, but not numerically identical with, the animality which is the essence of the essence of every other animal. The genus is the class of these essences. It follows from this class theory that a universal is not a word but a real thing, not a status of individuals but something transcending individuals, not an unchanging eternal idea but something constantly changing. The humanity which exists today, the class of the essences of men now living, is not the humanity which existed a thousand years ago or even yesterday, yet it is identical with it; humanity retains its identity just as a growing organism retains its identity through all its changes. Thus the class theory taught that humanity is not a concept but a living thing.

## ABELARD AS A DIALECTICIAN

These speculations marked the beginning of a new epoch in the intellectual history of Europe. No longer satisfied with repeating the few fragments which had been handed down from ancient philosophy, scholars boldly sought to grow in wisdom by exercising their own rational powers. Men of talent who a generation earlier would have followed a military career now found in philosophy a nobler arena for contest. Abelard was the most brilliant example of the new intellectual enthusiasm.

Born in 1079 at Palais, near Nantes in Brittany, Peter Abelard was destined to follow the career of his father, a knight, but was first sent to school for a liberal education. He found his studies so fascinating that, as he says in his autobiography, leaving to his brothers the pomp of military glory together with his inheritance and rights of primogeniture, he deserted the court of Mars for the bosom of Minerva. He did not, however, give up the spirit of knighthood. Putting on the armor of dialectic, he became a knight-errant of philosophy. Wandering from one province to another, ready to challenge all comers in dialectical combat, he became known among scholars as "the Peripatetic of Palais."

After studying under various teachers, including Roscelin, who was now teaching again after his return from England, Abelard finally came to the intellectual capital, Paris, and enrolled in the class of William of Champeaux at the cathedral school. At first he was welcomed as a brilliant student, but his constant talking in class and persistent attempts to refute the lecturer soon irritated both the professor and the older students. When the situation had become intolerable, Abelard, with unheard of presumption for one so young, announced the establishment of a rival school of his own at Melun, twenty-five miles from Paris. The new school, which was supported by some of William's political enemies, attracted so many students that Abelard's reputation as a teacher began to eclipse William's. Emboldened by success, he determined to lay siege to the capital, and moved his school to Corbeil, nearer Paris, from where he could easily send students to attack William in his classroom. The siege was suddenly raised, however, when a spell of ill health brought on by overstudy compelled Abelard to go home to Palais.

Some years later, having recovered his health, Abelard returned to the fray. William was now teaching at the monastery of St. Victor. Resolving to make a direct assault, Abelard again enrolled in his class, and finally succeeded in compelling William to admit the falsity of the essence theory he had been teaching. This capitulation left Abelard master of the dialectical field. William, known as the professor who had been refuted in his own classroom, found his classes deserted as the students flocked to Abelard's standard. William's successor at the cathedral school, recognizing the situation, abdicated in favor of Abelard, and became himself a student in the class he had just been teaching. William, furious, obtained this man's expulsion and had one of his own protégés appointed to the chair. This move forced Abelard to withdraw to Melun, where he reestablished his old school. Not long after, William left Paris together with his followers. No sooner had he gone than Abelard returned. In order to besiege, as he says, the enemy entrenched at the cathedral, he pitched his camp on Mount St. Genevieve—thus establishing the tradition of that "Latin Quarter" which soon became the intellectual center of Europe. William, hastening back to St. Victor to raise the siege, only succeeded in attracting to himself all his protégé's students, so that the latter was forced to give up teaching and became a monk in despair. Although Goswin, a disciple of Joscelin, advocate of the class theory, is said to have conducted a successful raid against Abelard's classroom, the principal battle now raged between the schools of St. Genevieve and St. Victor, and Abelard was fully satisfied with his own success in it. He finally left Paris on an errand of piety, to visit his mother, who, following her husband's example, was about to enter a convent; soon after, William also left to become bishop of Chalons.

Besides several minor works Abelard composed three general textbooks of logic. Each is extant only in part and in a single manuscript. Of the earliest, known from its first word as the *Logic "Ingredientibus,"* the manuscript includes commentaries on Porphyry's *Introduction,* Aristotle's *Categories,* and Aristotle's *De interpretatione.* Of the second, the *Logic "Nostrorum petitioni sociorum,"* we have only the commentary on Porphyry. The latest, called the *Dialectic,* has the form, not of a commentary on the classics, but of an original textbook of logic, and this presumably represents Abelard's definitive doctrine.

The place of the problem of universals in a twelfth-century course on logic is at the very beginning. The course begins with a discussion of Porphyry's *Introduction,* and Porphyry begins with his reference to the problem of universals. The *Logic "Ingredientibus"* opens, consequently, with a thorough treatment of this problem. In the *Logic "Nostrorum petitioni sociorum"* the discussion of universals is fragmentary and often obscure, owing undoubtedly to flaws in the manuscript. In the only manuscript of the *Dialectic* the first part of the work, which presumably included Abelard's final formulation of his theory of universals, is lacking altogether. We are therefore compelled to study his theory from his earliest work on it, and it remains uncertain to what extent he may have modified his views later.

## ABELARD'S THEORY OF UNIVERSALS

### Criticism of the Realist Theories

In studying the nature of genera and species as typical universals, we must first inquire, says Abelard,[7] whether they pertain only to words or also to things. The classical authorities use phrases which seem to imply that universals are both significant words and signified things. Let us consider how either a single thing or a collection of things could be universal, that is, predicated separately of many individuals.

Some understand by the reality of the universal that a substance essentially the same exists in individuals differing from each other by their accidental forms, and likewise in species differing from each other by their specific differences. Whatever authority may be alleged for this theory, it is refuted by the facts of science. If it were true, then the animal informed by rationality would be identical with the animal informed by irrationality, and so the rational animal would be an irrational animal, and thus contraries would coexist in the same thing or rather would no longer be contraries. Rationality and irrationality would coexist even in Socrates, because the rational man Socrates would be identical with the irrational ass Burnellus if whatever is in Socrates besides the forms of Socrates, namely, Socrates himself, is identical with that which is in Burnellus besides the forms of Burnellus, namely, Burnellus himself. This conclusion cannot be avoided by saying that the proposition *The rational animal is the irrational animal* is true insofar as the animal is rational for one reason and irrational for another, namely, the opposed forms; for when we say, for example, *The rational animal is the mortal animal,* we mean that the animal is rational for one reason and mortal for another, but that the two forms coexist without opposition. Furthermore, according to this theory there would be only ten essences altogether, namely, the ten summa genera (Aristotle's "categories"). Just as all substances would in the last analysis be essentially one, so all qualities would be essentially one, all quantities would be essentially one, and so of the others. Socrates possesses a certain quality, a certain quantity, and so forth; so does Plato. But if there is only one quality, then the quality of Socrates is identical with that of Plato, and similarly of the other accidents. Therefore Socrates and Plato would have identically the same accidents, and so could not differ by their accidental forms any more than by their substance. Furthermore, even if men did differ in form, they would not for that reason be numerically many, for we do not call Socrates numerically many because he acquires many forms. Furthermore, if individuals derived their being from their own accidents, as the theory maintains, then their accidents would be prior to themselves. From all these considerations (presumably the same by which Abelard forced William to recant) it is clear that the essence theory is utterly irrational.

Other realists admit, therefore, that individual things are not only different from each other by their forms but personally discrete in their essences, and that what is in one, whether matter or form, is nowise in the other, and that they would be no less distinct in their essences if all forms were removed, because their personal discreteness, through which this one is not that one, is not produced by forms but by an actual difference of essence. Otherwise the difference of forms would involve an infinite regress, since each difference of forms would require still other forms to explain it. But these realists insist that things both materially and formally discrete, although not the same *essentially,* nevertheless may be the same *indifferently.* Men are discrete in themselves but the same in man, that is, do not differ in the nature of humanity. The same men are individual through discreteness but universal through indifference and likeness.

There are two forms of this theory. Some assume that the only universal thing is a class of individuals; all men collected together constitute the species man, and all animals collected together constitute the genus animal. Others say that any individual man, insofar as he is man, is species, and is predicated of many in the sense of agreeing with many.

The class theory is refuted as follows: (1) Granted that the class is predicated of many *partially,* this has nothing to do with the commonness of the universal, which is in each individual *completely,* this being precisely the difference between a universal and a whole. (2) Socrates, having many parts, would in this sense be predicated of many, and so be himself a universal. (3) Any group of men would constitute a species. (4) Any group of bodies and spirits would constitute one universal substance. The whole class of substances is one summum genus, but by taking away any one we could form many summa genera among substances, for if the remaining substances did not constitute a summum genus they would have to be a species of substance contrasted with some co-ordinate species. (5) A universal is naturally prior to its particulars, but a class is posterior to the members of which it is composed. (6) The species is the same as its genus, but the part is not the same as its whole; man is animal, but the class of men is not the class of animals.

The other theory (the indifference theory) is equally untenable. According to it, individuals are called universal insofar as they agree with others, and to be predicated of many does not mean being many essentially but merely agreeing with many. But if to be predicated is to agree, we cannot say the individual is that which is predicated of one thing only, since nothing agrees with one thing only. We cannot distinguish at all between universal and partic-ular. Man as man and Socrates as man agree with others, but neither man as Socrates nor Socrates as Socrates agrees with others; so whatever is said of man is said likewise of Socrates, and in the same way. Socrates and the man which is in Socrates are indistin-guishable, because nothing can differ from itself. Moreover, Socrates does not agree with Plato either in matter or in form. If you say he agrees with him in the *thing* which is man, but man is no thing except Socrates or somebody else, then he must agree with Plato either in himself (in which he differs from him) or in somebody else (which even he himself is not). If you say he agrees only *negatively* in not differing, that is, that Socrates does not differ from Plato in man, you can say equally well that he does not differ from him in stone, since neither of them is a stone, and so you have as much reason to call them stones as to call them men. But it is false that they do not differ in man, for if Socrates does not differ from Plato in the thing which is man, then he does not differ from Plato in himself; it is precisely in the thing which is man, that is, in himself, that he does differ from Plato.

These arguments demonstrate that things (*res*), whether taken singly or collectively, cannot be called universal in the sense of being predicated of many.

### Exposition of the Nominalist Theory

It is necessary, therefore, to ascribe universality to words (*voces* or *vocabula*) alone.[8] Just as grammarians classify nouns (*nomina*) as common and proper, so logicians classify simple terms (*sermones*) as universal and particular (or singular). A word is universal which is designed to be predicated separately of many, as the noun *man,* which can be joined to the particular names of men because of their nature. A word is singular which is predicated of only one, as *Socrates,* which is the name of one person only.

The universal, then, is *that which is predicated of many*. The *that which* indicates the simplicity of the term, as distinguished from spoken utterances, and the unity of its meaning, as distinguished from homonymous words. The *is predicated* means to be joinable to something veraciously by virtue of the enunciation of the copulative verb in the present tense. The *of many* refers to a diversity of things denoted, not to various ways of understanding the same thing.

Universal words, thus defined, do not signify things according to their distinctness, for then they would not be universal, nor things as agreeing in something, for there is no thing in which they do agree, nor a class of things, for a proposition about the universal may hold of one individual only (as, *A man is sitting here*). They seem, therefore, to signify nothing, and consequently to produce understanding about nothing. But this does not follow. Universal words denote particular things in a certain way, and they produce an understanding pertaining to these things, not transcending them. The word *man* denotes individuals for the common reason that they are men, and it produces a certain common understanding pertaining to the individuals whose common likeness it conceives.

In order to understand this, we must solve three problems: (1) what is that common cause on account of which the universal name is imposed? (2) what is the understanding's common conception of the likeness of things? and (3) is the word called common because of the common cause in which things agree or because of the common conception or because of both?

(1) Individual men, although differing from each other both in their forms and in their essences, nevertheless agree in that they are men. They do not agree in *man,* because man is always an individual, but in *being a man. To be a man* is not a man or any *thing;* it is the *status* of a thing. The status of man is made up of those things, stationed in man's nature, whose common likeness is conceived by whoever imposes the name. The status is not an essence and may be purely negative. Different things agree when they individually either are the same or are not the same. Socrates and Plato, who, as has been shown, do not agree in any thing, do agree in their status. They are called men because each is a man, that is, has the status *being a man,* just as a horse and an ass are called non-men because each is not a man, that is, has the status *not being a man*. This common status of individual things, by which they agree with each other, is the cause for imposing a universal name on them.

(2) Understanding, an action of the soul, differs from sense in not requiring either a corporeal instrument or a corporeal object.

Its object may be either a perceived body or a fictitious image constructed by the mind in the likeness of some body. The understanding produced by a particular word conceives the proper and particular form of one individual, while that produced by a universal word conceives a common and confused image of many individuals. The word *Socrates* names and determines one thing. The word *man* names many things but determines none. The object of the understanding in this case is the common form, which retains the likeness of many things, although in itself it is one thing. When not founded on experience, these conceived forms do not correspond to the true natures of things, which are known only to God, who created things according to their preconceived forms. Names of existing things may produce understanding, because they are applied in accordance with some natures or properties of things, although imperfectly; but names of the insensible intrinsic forms of things, such as rationality or mortality, can only produce opinion. These imaginary forms, to which the action of the understanding is directed, are precisely what the universal words signify. As forms conceived in the mind universals exist apart from sensible bodies, although as words predicated of many they exist only in them; they exist in themselves naturally, in their particulars actually. The conceived form is neither thing, of which it is the likeness, nor understanding, of which it is the object, but a third sort of entity, which can be described as the meaning of a word.

(3) The universal word is called common both because of the common cause of its imposition, that is, the common status in which things naturally agree, and because of the common conception which it produces in the mind—but primarily for the former reason.

Our understanding of universals, therefore, is a process of abstraction. Abstraction is a way of understanding, not a way of subsisting. In abstraction we consider separately some one status of things which does not subsist separately but in conjunction with others. We conceive this status not as separate but separately. To conceive it as separate would be false, since it does not subsist as separate. But to conceive it separately gives true, although incomplete, understanding, since it is actually in the thing, although it is not everything which is in the thing. So far as we abstract from things properties which they actually possess, we have true understanding concerning them. But the understanding of universals is always *apart* and *bare* and *pure*—apart from sense, because it does not perceive the thing as sensual; bare with reference to its abstraction from some or all forms; perfectly pure with respect to discreteness, because no thing, whether matter or form, is determined by this sort of confused conception.

## Summary

Abelard's theory avoids the realist and nominalist extremes by maintaining that the universal is neither a thing nor a concept but a logical term which is related both to things and to concepts. The universal itself is a word, but a word for the universality of which there exist definite grounds. The subjective ground is the common, that is, confused, concept which it evokes in the understanding and which is, strictly speaking, its meaning. But the primary ground is the common status of the things denoted. The ground of the universal, therefore, is objective but not real, for in Latin to be *real* means to be a thing (*res*) and that which is common is not a thing but the status of a thing. This *status theory,* as it might be called, is radically opposed to the Aristotelian doctrine that the specific form is objectively the most essential and subjectively the most intelligible aspect of things. For Abelard the common status is not essential and the common concept is always confused.

## ABELARD AS A THEOLOGIAN

When he returned from Brittany, Abelard resolved to study theology, under the celebrated professor Anselm of Laon. Like a tree of magnificent foliage but no fruit, says Abelard, he talked fluently but explained nothing. As Abelard began to cut class more and more frequently, the other students became indignant, and when he assured them that he could understand theology without the aid of such lectures, they challenged him to give a lecture himself. They chose a difficult passage in Ezekiel, and he agreed to expound it to them the very next day. He expounded it so successfully that his hearers were charmed and urged him to continue to lecture to them. But as these extracurricular classes became more and more popular, Anselm intervened and compelled him to leave Laon.

His reputation, however, was now established, and he was offered again his former chair at the Paris cathedral school. Here for several years he taught dialectic and theology, and grew in fame and wealth as the students crowded his classroom. Abelard, thirty-eight years old, was now at the summit of his career. Swollen with pride, he considered himself the only philosopher in the world, and felt only one thing lacking to make his felicity complete.

Abelard had always been celibate. His studies had left him no time for social activities, and his refined tastes found nothing attractive in the girls who hung around the schools. But in the adolescent niece of his fellow canon Fulbert he now found a girl whom he considered worthy of his love. Heloise was remarkable both for her beauty and for her scholarship. Abelard plotted a campaign against her in the same romantic spirit in which he planned his dialectical battles. He persuaded Fulbert to take him into his house as a lodger by agreeing to tutor Heloise in his spare

time. Abelard confesses his amazement at the naïveté with which
the unsuspecting Fulbert committed his tender lamb to the care
of a hungry wolf. His autobiography describes his method of tutor-
ing briefly but vividly. When Heloise's condition could no longer
be concealed, he secretly sent her away to his relatives in Brittany,
where their son Astralabius was born, and where the visit of the
learned Parisian beauty so impressed the simple peasants that she
lived on as a sorceress in the Breton folklore. Meanwhile Abelard
tried to appease her furious uncle by offering to marry her. Fulbert
had been the last to suspect what was going on in his own house;
long before he discovered it, Abelard's love songs to Heloise were
being sung throughout Paris and his students were complaining
that he was neglecting his studies to such an extent that he simply
repeated his old lectures. The marriage proposal, however, was
rejected by Heloise, who, with absolute devotion to Abelard's interests, described in detail the many disadvantages to a philosopher
of having a wife. Abelard insisted, and they agreed on a secret
marriage. But Fulbert violated the secret, and his resulting quar-
rels with Heloise, who stoutly denied the marriage, made it intolerable for her to continue to live in his house. Abelard therefore
placed her temporarily in the convent of Argenteuil, where she had
been educated. Fulbert, in the mistaken belief that he was trying
to get rid of her, was so enraged that, with the assistance of some
relatives, he assaulted and emasculated Abelard. Plunged at one
stroke from the height of felicity and fame to the depth of misery
and shame, Abelard was so overwhelmed by confusion and despair
that he became a monk, while Heloise likewise took the veil at
Argenteuil.

Abelard entered the celebrated Benedictine monastery of St.
Denis near Paris. This was his first acquaintance with twelfth-
century monastic life, and he was deeply scandalized by the im-
morality of the monks. The new novice, he himself says, "rebuked

them for their intolerable obscenities frequently and vehemently, both in private and in public," and this soon made him, as one might expect, "exceedingly burdensome and hateful to them all." When the theology students urged that he be allowed to leave the monastery in order to continue his teaching, the abbot consented with alacrity, and Abelard and his new brethren parted with mutual pleasure.

He withdrew to a place in the country. The students who flocked there to follow his courses on theology and other subjects came in such numbers that they could not find food or lodging. His popularity aroused the envy of the established professors, especially Alberic and Lotulf of Rheims, who had succeeded William of Champeaux and Anselm of Laon, both now dead, as the respectable authorities on theology. When Abelard published a book *On the Divine Unity and Trinity,* they caused a council to be summoned at Soissons for the purpose of declaring it heretical. No heresy could be discovered, and Abelard was acquitted. His enemies, however, persuaded the presiding legate to condemn the book on the sole ground that it had been published without the ecclesiastical imprimatur. Abelard was sentenced to burn the manuscript with his own hand, to recite the Athanasian creed like a Sunday-school boy, and to be imprisoned in the monastery of St. Medard (where his jailor, the prior, was his old opponent Goswin). He always considered this undeserved humiliation as an even worse blow than his former disaster, but confessed that it was a divine retribution for his pride, as that had been for his lust.

The imprisonment was soon remitted, however, and Abelard was sent back to the scarcely less uncongenial environment of his own monastery. He now went in for scholarly research. The first fruit of these studies was the discovery of a proof that St. Denis, founder of the monastery and patron of France, was not the real St. Denis, St. Paul's disciple Dionysius the Areopagite, but another man of the same name. Abelard literally had to flee for his life. Negotiations to extradite him from his sanctuary in the country were under way when the abbot providentially died. The new abbot, Suger, who later reformed the monastery, gave Abelard permission to live anywhere he wanted, provided he did not become subject to any other monastery.

Deciding now to become a hermit, he withdrew to a desolate wilderness, where he built himself a little oratory of reeds, and he found such consolation in the peace of this retreat that he named it the Paraclete, that is, Consoler. But the irrepressible students pursued him even to the wilderness. Compelling him to resume his teaching, they formed a little community of hermits living on the simplest fare in tents around the oratory, which they rebuilt of wood and stone on a larger scale. Again Abelard's fame as a teacher spread through western Christendom. But he found the Paraclete less and less consoling as he realized that the leaders of monastic society were openly questioning his orthodoxy. He began to dream darkly of fleeing to some heathen land far away. But suddenly an unexpected opportunity for escape was offered by an invitation to become abbot of the monastery of St. Gildas in Brittany. So he left his Paraclete. Some time later, when the nuns of Argenteuil were evicted by a foreclosure, he deeded it to them. Heloise was made abbess, and under her efficient administration it became a prosperous convent.

The new abbot of St. Gildas found the monks over whom he had come to rule more barbarous than any heathen. The local lord confiscated the abbey's land and laid ambushes to slay the abbot. The monks stole all the money in the treasury for their concubines, and then demanded more from Abelard. His efforts to enforce the Benedictine *Rule* failed completely. When he expelled rebellious brethren, they refused to go. The monks were constantly plotting to murder him, both by poison and by the sword. After barely escaping several attempts on his life, Abelard resigned.

He now enjoyed a few years of freedom, which he devoted to teaching and writing. For a while he resumed his lectures on Mount St. Genevieve. For the nuns of the Paraclete he wrote hymns and sermons, as well as a modification of the Benedictine *Rule* suitable for the use of women. The final edition of his theology was probably made at this time.

Abelard's extant works include three general treatises on theology—*On the Divine Unity and Trinity, Christian Theology,* and *Introduction to Theology*. They agree in doctrine and to a considerable extent in words, being three editions rather than three books. The Latin is easy but verbose and marked by interminable digressions and repetitions. The explanation of the doctrine of the Trinity, the principal subject of all three, is given most fully in the second. *Yes and No (Sic et non)*, a learned collection of citations from the Fathers of the Church arranged by topics, is a source book of dogmatic theology in which the authorities for each proposition are followed by the authorities against it, reconciliation of the contradictions being left entirely to the reader. *Know Thyself (Scito teipsum)* contains Abelard's ethical doctrine. Other theological works are an account of the six days of creation, a commentary on Romans, a dialogue between a philosopher, a Christian, and a Jew, and several minor works. The following section will summarize the principal doctrines found in these books.

Besides these theological works and the logical works already mentioned, Abelard wrote an autobiography (called *A Story of Calamities*), a rule for Benedictine nuns, and a number of sermons. His love songs being lost, his only extant poetical works are a didactic poem addressed to Astralabius and a number of hymns. The celebrated *Letters of Abelard and Heloise,* the authenticity of which has long been disputed, were probably published by Abelard, whether or not they represent exactly the actual correspondence.

## ABELARD'S THEOLOGY

### *Faith and Understanding*

The Catholic faith consists of two parts, one concerning the nature of divinity itself, the other concerning the divine benefits and ordinances. To believe its doctrines is necessary for salvation. To understand them is not necessary. Neither is it possible, for God's acts are not subject to the laws of science, and God's nature is not subject to the laws of logic. Even if it were possible, it would not be desirable. Authority is preferable to human reason in all matters, and especially in those pertaining to God we rely on authority more safely than on human judgment. To have merit with God we must believe in God as he speaks through the saints, not believe in our fallible little human reasons. Of course we must understand the doctrines of faith sufficiently to know what the words mean, otherwise faith itself would be impossible. But we need not understand them in the sense of being able to prove them rationally. We believe in order that we may know, but understanding is not knowing. Understanding and faith are two ways of imperfectly apprehending invisible things. Knowledge is the experience of visible things. The knowledge of God for the sake of which we now believe in him will be possible only when we have direct vision of him by being in his presence.

Nevertheless, in spite of the fact that it is neither necessary nor possible, we are obliged to endeavor to understand rationally the doctrines which we believe, and especially the fundamental doctrine of the Trinity. This is because it is the duty of theology not only to teach the Catholic faith but also to defend it against its enemies. The faith will never need new teachers. The Fathers have established its doctrines and they are its teachers forever. But it will always need new defenders. Every age produces new heresies, and consequently the Catholic theologians of every age must provide new defenses against heresy. Our own age, the twelfth century, has produced a crop of heresies equal to that of any of its predecessors. Some of them can be refuted easily, but one is particularly dangerous. This is the rationalism of the self-styled "philosophers," modern successors of the sophists denounced by Plato, who attack Christianity with fallacious dialectical arguments. It is in order to defend our faith against their rational, or rather irrational, attacks that we are obliged to understand it rationally. We must *answer a fool according to his folly,* and overcome the enemy by means of his own weapons.[9]

The weapons with which the faith is defended against pseudophilosophy and pseudo-dialectic are true philosophy and true dialectic. Heresies can be overcome only by argument, not by force. Ordinary heretics, who acknowledge at least some authority, can be refuted by an appeal to the authority they acknowledge. But the rationalists, who acknowledge no authority save that of the human reason, can be refuted only by human reason. This is why we must study philosophy and especially dialectic. Christian monks should not be forbidden to study these subjects, nor, for that matter, any other sciences. Such prohibitions are only devised by ignorant men as a solace for their own ignorance. Far from being opposed to Christianity, philosophy and logic are identical with it. *Logic* is the study of *Logos; philosophy* is the love of *Sophia; Christianity* is the religion of *Christ.* Since Christ is the true Sophia and Logos, to be a Christian, to be a philosopher, and to be a logician are synonymous phrases.[10]

The endeavor to understand God by dialectic can succeed to a considerable extent. We cannot comprehend the divine nature by reason any more than by faith. Incomprehensible and ineffable because he transcends our ways of thinking or speaking, God can be described only in figures of speech. Even Plato, when speaking of "the Good," did not dare to say what it is, for concerning it he only knew that what it is cannot be known by men. We cannot rigidly demonstrate even God's existence or unity, let alone his Trinity, by necessary proofs capable of compelling the assent of obstinate infidels. But the evidence given by nature for its creator and ruler makes God's existence sufficiently obvious to any reasonable man, and the moral necessity of postulating his existence is the most cogent sort of proof for any moral man. As to the Trinity, we can show that, when considered rationally, it is the most plausible doctrine. This is all that is necessary, since we are not teaching the faith by reason but merely defending it.

If the doctrine of the Trinity can be understood, even imperfectly, by reason alone without any appeal to faith or authority, then it must have actually been so understood by men endowed with reason but not faith, and notably by the wise men of the pre-Christian era before the faith had been revealed. We find that as a matter of fact the doctrine of the Trinity was not originated by Christ but was taught by both the sacred and the profane writers of antiquity.[11] Turning to the Old Testament, we find many references to the Trinity, beginning with the very first verse, *In the beginning God created the heaven and the earth,* which, by its ungrammatical conjunction of the singular verb *creavit* with the plural subject *Eloim* (gods), mistranslated by the Latin singular *Deus,* can only signify that God is both one and many. Turning to the pagan philosophers, we find that they have taught the Trinity ever since Hermes, the most ancient philosopher we know. The Christian doctrine is most clearly set forth in the books of the Platonists, who call the Father "the Good," the Son "the Mind," and the Holy Ghost "the World Soul." The Platonic

World Soul means the cosmic soul by which our souls are animated spiritually; this is precisely the Christian doctrine of the Holy Ghost, who "proceeds" in two ways—eternally and affectively from the Father and Son as the third person of the Trinity, temporally and effectively from God to creation as the spiritual animator of men. We see, therefore, that the doctrine of the Trinity, which constitutes our faith concerning the nature of divinity itself, actually has been, and so still can be, arrived at by reason alone.

## The Trinity

There are three necessary and sufficient conditions of the highest good. It must be perfectly powerful, perfectly wise, and perfectly benevolent. Any two of these without the third would be futile, so all are necessary. Every other attribute of the good can be subsumed under some one of these three, so they are sufficient. It is obvious, therefore, that the highest good, which we call God, is a Trinity, since it consists in three persons, God omnipotent, God omniscient, and God omnibenevolent—all three being one identical God.[12]

God's omnipotence is compatible with the determinism of his action, his omniscience is compatible with the free choice of creatures, and his omnibenevolence is compatible with the existence of evil. God's omnipotence does not mean that he is able to do anything. Ability to do something unworthy of him would be a weakness, not a power, just as in a man to *be able* to lose a battle is a weakness, not a power. Omnipotence means that he is able to do whatever he wills and that nothing can resist his will. His will is strictly determined by his omniscience and omnibenevolence. Being wise and benevolent he always wills, and being omnipotent consequently does, that which is in fact the best. Since he could not possibly will other than he actually does will, it follows from the very fact of his omnipotence that he could not possibly do other than he actually does do. God's omniscience does not imply the denial of contingency in the world. Unlike God, man has free choice in the sense of being able to change his mind after deliberation, and so is able to choose either of two alternatives. The actual choice is the cause, not the effect, of God's foreknowledge of it. What God has foreseen necessarily happens, but this does not imply that what God has foreseen happens necessarily. A thing *can* happen otherwise than God has foreseen it *would* happen, but it *cannot* happen otherwise than he has foreseen it *could* happen, and it *does not* happen otherwise than he has foreseen it *would* happen. God's omnibenevolence does not exclude evil. His will is manifested in one of two ways, by disposing or by counseling. He always disposes and counsels well. What he disposes well is necessarily accomplished well. But what he counsels well may be rejected by the sinful free creature, and the consequent evil is permitted, although not willed, by God.

The "dialecticians" object that it is logically impossible for the three persons to be simultaneously both the same as each other and different from each other, as the doctrine of the Trinity requires. Their objection only shows that they have not studied dialectic. Dialectic teaches us that there are many meanings of *same* and *different*. Besides various extended meanings of the word *same,* as when we call two things the same in the sense of *similar,* as two individuals of a species or two species of a genus, or when we call two things the same in the sense of *equivalent,* as having the same value or the same effect, or when we call a thing the same in the sense of *immutable,* as being always the same, there are four strict meanings of the word *same,* and correspondingly of its opposite *different.* Two things may be the same or different in *number,* in *essence,* in *property,* or in *definition.*[13]

Things are the *same in number* when they are only one thing.

They are different in number when they are two or more things. Things which are discrete from each other in the whole extent of their essence are different in number. Things generically, specifically, or individually distinct are equally different in number. Socrates and Plato, having no part in common (according to the nominalist theory), are different in number, that is, they are two men; they are not one anything; they are the same only in similarity, both being men. Things which through sharing any part are included in each other wholly or partly are the same in number. This hand and this man are the same in number, because they cannot be added up to make two anything; they are only one thing.

Things which are the same in number are also the *same in essence* when they are identically the same thing in the whole extent of their essence. They are different in essence when they share each other's essence only in part, and so are not the same thing. This hand and this man are different in essence, because, although only one thing, they are not the same thing. This hand is not this man, and this man is not this hand. But this wax and this image are the same in essence. The wax and the image are identical in every part of their extent; the wax is the waxen image, and the image is the waxen image.

Things which are the same in essence are also the *same in property* (or predication) when each participates in all the properties of the other and so each can be predicated of the other. They are different in property when their properties are so incompatible that one cannot participate in the property of the other. In a waxen image the matter—namely, the wax—and the product made out of it—namely, the image—although the same in essence, are different in property, because the matter is not the product, that is, the wax itself is not made out of the wax, and the product is not the matter, that is, the image itself is not the matter of the image. But that white object and that hard object are the same in property because the white object, being hard, participates in the hard object's property hardness, and the hard object, being white, participates in the white object's property whiteness, and so each can be predicated of the other—that white object is that hard object, and that hard object is that white object.

Things which are the same in property are also the *same in definition* when to be either one is to be the other, so that whatever is either is for that very reason also the other. They are different in definition when their properties do not imply each other. That white object and that hard object are different in definition, because being the one does not imply being the other. But the bright object and the shiny object [14] are the same in definition, because to be bright is to be shiny, and conversely.

The three persons of the Trinity are the same in number and in essence (as well as in all the extended meanings of *same*), but different in definition and in property.[15]

They are the same in number because there is only one God. The highest good must surpass all other goods and therefore be one and unique.

They are the same in essence because, God having no parts, whatever is God must be all of God. Not strictly speaking a substance but beyond substance, he has, unlike creatures, no diversity of parts or forms. Omnipotence, omniscience, and omnibenevolence are the same thing, God, in the whole extent of the divine essence, and so are the same in essence.

They are different in definition because to be omnipotent is not to be omniscient or omnibenevolent, or conversely. God has numberless attributes—he is powerful, wise, just, eternal, merciful, and so forth; and all these are different in definition.

They are different in property (or predication) because of the incompatible properties of omnipotence, omniscience, and omnibenevolence. *Person* means more than *attribute*—else God would be as many persons as he is attributes; *person* means an attribute so incompatible in property with another as not to be predicable of that other. Omnipotence has all properties which pertain to power, including independence, the power of being of itself alone, technically called being *unbegotten,* and omniscience, the power of discerning perfectly. Omniscience, the power of discerning perfectly, has the property of being a particular power, and therefore derived from power. Omnibenevolence has the property of proceeding from omnipotence and omniscience in its effect, for the will to accomplish what is best presupposes the power to accomplish and the knowledge of what is best. In accordance with the philosophical terminology which calls species the "procreations" of the genus which includes them, omniscience, a species of power, is called the *Son* of the omnipotence which includes it, and is said to be *begotten* by omnipotence as being of its substance, and the latter, consequently, is called the *Father* who *begets* it. The divine emotion of benevolence is called the Holy *Spirit* because emotions are manifested by "spirit" or breath—as love by sighing or pain by groaning. It follows from the foregoing that the Father is unbegotten and begets the Son, that the Son is begotten by the Father, and that the Holy Ghost proceeds from the Father and the Son. These properties are incompatible, therefore the three persons are different in property, and cannot be predicated of each other. The Father is not the Son or Holy Ghost; the Son is not the Father or Holy Ghost; and the Holy Ghost is not the Father or Son. They each participate in all the divine attributes, even in each other's special attributes; each person is omnipotent, omniscient, and omnibenevolent. But they do not participate in each other; the Father is omniscient but not omniscience, that is, the Son; he is omnibenevolent but not omnibenevolence, that is the Holy Ghost; and so of the others. This difference implies no difference in essence. Even the Holy Ghost, who is not, like the Son, of the Father's substance, is nevertheless of the same substance with the Father and the Son. And it implies no separateness in operation. Each person does what the others do, but is not as the others are.

Ordinary experience provides many examples of things related in this way, same in number and essence, different in definition and property. Anselm of Canterbury's analogy of a spring, a stream arising from it, and a pond fed by them, which are not each other although they are the same water (with the analogy extended to the incarnation by enclosing the stream in a pipe), is not quite exact, because the same water is not spring, stream, and pond simultaneously. A better analogy is the sun's substance, brilliance, and luminosity. But the most perfect analogy for confounding the pseudo-philosophers is that of a bronze seal, in which its material, the bronze, its form, the royal image, and its act, sealing the wax, are related to each other exactly as the persons of the Trinity are.

## Ethics

Charity is treated in Abelard's book *Know Thyself*, which, following the Psalmist's summary of ethics, *Depart from evil and do good,* is divided in two parts, the first dealing with evil and the second with good. Only the first part is extant.

We sin only in what we do voluntarily. So-called original sin is not sin, strictly speaking, but the penalty of sin. Our first parents alone are guilty of this sin, but we all inherit the penalty of it. In baptism God remits the penalty but not the guilt, because there is no guilt in the infant.

Sin does not consist in any act. The act of committing murder or adultery or any other evil deed is not sin, for such acts can be done entirely without sin under certain circumstances, as through force or fraud or ignorance. Nor does sin consist in the carnal pleasure which attends evil acts. Such pleasures are natural, and therefore not sinful. Nor does sin consist in the consequences of acting, which are morally irrelevant. Judas' sin is not mitigated by the good consequences which followed. Nor does sin consist in ignorance, which is a defect of the mind, but not a moral defect. Those who killed Christ and the martyrs in the mistaken opinion that they were criminals did not sin, but rather would have sinned had they failed to kill them. Nor does sin consist in vice. Vice, a moral defect of the mind, such as wrathfulness or lustfulness, inclines us to sin, but, far from being sin, provides the very material for conflict which makes the triumph of virtue possible. Nor does sin consist in bad will, which is present without sin when the malevolence is resisted and absent with sin when we choose the worse alternative of a moral dilemma without willing either. Indeed bad will is a necessary condition of merit, which consists in resisting our own bad will in order to fulfill God's good will. Nor does sin consist in disobedience to God's command, which is not necessarily sinful. When Christ, after curing the deaf and dumb man, *charged them that they should tell no man,* they disobeyed, but for his honor, not in contempt, and so without sin.

Sin consists only in the bad intention whereby we consent to our bad will and resolve to commit the evil deed if possible, thereby offending God by contempt. Men judge according to the manifest deed, but God judges according to the hidden intention. Carrying out a good or bad intention adds nothing to its moral merit or demerit, and two men whose intentions are the same have the same merit, even though one is prevented from performing the intended act. But the intention is good or bad, and so meritorious or sinful, only when it is really good or bad, not when, through moral blindness, it is wrongly thought to be so. Moral ignorance of what is pleasing and displeasing to God must not be confused with the ignorance of fact which may cause an evil deed to be committed with a good intention and therefore without sin. We are responsible before God, and rewarded or punished by him, neither for what we are nor for what we desire nor for what we do but for what we intend.

Reconciliation after sinning is accomplished by penitence, the mind's remorse over its sin. True penitence, which is inspired by love of God, and which abhors the sin, not the penalty, wipes out the sin, that is, the consent to evil and contempt of God, together with its eternal penalty, though not its temporal penalty. Since love of God is incompatible with contempt of God, no one is truly penitent unless he repents of all his sins together.

Contrasted to the vices which incline us to evil deeds, the bad will by which we desire to commit them, the intention to commit them if possible, and the act of committing them are the virtues which incline us to good deeds, the good will by which we desire to commit them, the intention to commit them if possible, and the act of committing them. Just as sin consists only in the bad intention, so merit consists only in the good intention. This alone is required of us by God and eternally rewarded by him, and this alone is true charity.

## ABELARD AND BERNARD

The boldness, novelty, and popularity of Abelard's theological views aroused great concern among the more conservative theologians. They looked for leadership to Bernard, abbot of Clairvaux, who about this time preached a sermon to the students at Paris on the advantages of the monastic over the scholastic life and returned to Clairvaux with a catch of twenty-one novices. He agreed to remonstrate with Abelard privately. But Abelard demanded a public hearing, and offered to defend himself before an assembly to be held at Sens if Bernard would also appear there. Bernard accepted the challenge after some hesitation. If the notable assembly of ecclesiastics and laymen, including the king, anticipated with pleasure this contest between the two most brilliant thinkers of the time, they were destined to be disappointed. When the council assembled, Bernard read a list of allegedly heretical passages from Abelard's works and summoned Abelard either to deny he had written them or to defend them or to recant them. Abelard, dismayed to find that his debate had become a trial, appealed to the pope and walked out of the council. The judges then condemned the disputed passages.

Abelard set out for Rome to prosecute his appeal. But meanwhile Bernard had hastily dispatched letters to Rome urging immediate confirmation of the council's verdict. Abelard was at Cluny, where he had stopped in the course of his journey, when he received news that the pope had confirmed the verdict, convicted him of heresy, ordered his books burned, and sentenced him to perpetual silence. Abelard's career was definitively closed, and he himself an outlaw. But he found a sympathetic protector in the saintly abbot of Cluny, Peter the Venerable. Under his guidance Abelard submitted to Rome, recanted his heresies, made his peace with Bernard, and became a monk of Cluny. Here he edified the brethren by his piety and by the wisdom of his now infrequent discourses. Within less than two years of the council of Sens, however, he died, in 1142. His remains were sent to the Paraclete to be buried by Heloise.

Bernard, with zealous exaggeration, accused Abelard of Arianism in distinguishing degrees in the Trinity, of Pelagianism in exalting free choice above grace, and of Nestorianism in excluding the human Christ from the Trinity. He called him a dragon, a forerunner of Antichrist, and author of a foolology.[16] While this bitter persecution of a fellow monk engaged, like himself, in defending the dogma of the Church can only be explained by the fundamental difference in their temperaments, it arose also from fundamental differences in their philosophies.

In their theology both Abelard and Bernard acknowledged the

rights of both faith and understanding. But they considered the relation between them in fundamentally different ways. Abelard, following Augustine and Anselm's tradition of "faith seeking understanding," considered that to understand the doctrines we believe, although necessary only for refuting pseudo-rationalists, is to some extent possible. Faith and understanding are two imperfect ways of apprehending the same truths. For Bernard faith and understanding have separate domains; we believe some things and understand others.[17] Each way of knowing is infallible in its own domain. Contrasted to them is the domain of opinion where, in the lack of either faith or understanding, certitude is impossible. The domain of faith includes, for example, the Trinity, the redemption, and baptism; that of understanding includes God, freedom, and immortality; and that of opinion includes angels, the immaculate conception, and the validity of illicit sacraments. From Bernard's point of view Abelard confused faith with understanding when he undertook to give a reason for the superrational doctrine of the Trinity, confused faith with opinion when he defined faith as a supposition concerning invisible things,[18] and confused understanding with opinion when he referred to his rational explanations as expounding the sense of his own opinion by plausible reasons.[19] From Abelard's point of view, to prefer understanding to faith is to exalt petty human reason above divine revelation, yet at the same time to refuse to defend the faith rationally is to fail in the theologian's duty. For Abelard theology is based on revelation and resorts to reason only for the sake of apologetic, whereas for Bernard theology begins with reason and proceeds to revelation only when the resources of reason have been exhausted.

In their concept of God both accepted the whole Catholic dogma unreservedly. But they considered the relation between God and creatures in fundamentally different ways. Abelard calls God *a being* (*essentia*); "he is called a being properly, a substance improperly" (*sive essentia dicatur, quod proprie dicitur, sive substantia, quod abusive*).[20] As such he is one being among others, although the most perfect and the creator of all others. Bernard calls God not *a being* but *being* or rather *be* (*esse*); "he is the be of himself and of all things" (*qui suum ipsius est et omnium esse*).[21] As such he is not one among others but the very act of existence of all things. Abelard's pluralism allows creatures a certain independence once they are created. Bernard's monism makes all things continuously dependent on God for their being; but he avoids pantheism by explaining that he means efficient, not material, being—"The maker of all things which are made is their being, but their causal, not material, being." (*Esse est ergo omnium quae facta sunt ipse factor eorum, sed causale, non materiale.*) [22] For Abelard the supreme *being* is a substantive; for Bernard it is a verb.

In their ethics both assert that man is saved or damned according to his good or bad intention, and that this is the most important thing. But they differ radically concerning the less important things, namely, the good or bad thoughts and desires which do not save or damn. Abelard had a legalistic view of ethics. Man is before a tribunal where only one question is at stake—innocent or guilty? If his intention is good, he is innocent. If his thoughts and desires are bad, that is irrelevant, or rather that is all the more to his credit, since his victory over these vices and temptations is all the more glorious. Bernard had a mystic view of ethics. Writing for monks about whose salvation he had no serious doubt, he was concerned not for their salvation but for the purity of their souls, that purity which is man's lost likeness of God, and the recovery of which alone makes possible the direct knowledge of God by mystical contemplation in this life. Pride and temptation corrupt that purity and so hinder the soul from seeing God. Abelard's ethics is summed up in his paradox: "It is no sin either to lust after another's wife or to lie with her, but only to consent to this lust or action." [23] Bernard's is summed up in his metaphor: "Thought is the skin of the soul, emotion the flesh of the soul, and intention the bone of the soul." [24] The mere thought of evil, like a discoloring of the skin, is a blemish in the soul; desire for evil, like a tumor infecting the flesh, is a disease of the soul; and consent to evil, like a disease penetrating to the bone, is the death of the soul. Right intention, conversely, is the soul's life, pure emotion is its health, and holy thought is its beauty. Bernard's ethics is based on psychological insight. Abelard's ethics, like his metaphysics and his theology, is based on logical analysis.

# Chapter IV. BERNARD OF CLAIRVAUX

## THE SPIRIT OF MONASTICISM

FROM the earliest days of Christianity there have been those who have taken it seriously, who have been willing to renounce the world in order to save their souls. Such Christians are called monks. Monasticism [1] is a life of systematic devotion to a more complete realization of man's supernatural end and to a closer conscious union of the soul with God, by the removal of every hindrance to this elevation of mind arising from self or external things and by the practice of the Christian virtues according to the evangelical counsels of poverty, chastity, and obedience. It has assumed various forms. The most spectacular monk was Simeon Stylites of Antioch, in the fifth century, who withdrew from the world vertically and lived thirty-seven years on top of a pillar. A more popular way of withdrawal was followed by the many hermits who imitated the famous fourth-century ascetic Anthony by fleeing to the deserts of Egypt, where, however, if we may believe the legends, they found plenty of temptations to combat. Others organized monastic societies where they followed the austere community life prescribed in the discipline attributed to Basil, bishop of Caesarea in Asia Minor in the fourth century.

In the Latin-speaking part of Christendom, monasticism was organized in a way congenial to the more restrained temperament of western Europeans by the *Rule* published in 529 by Benedict, founder of the monastery of Monte Cassino in southern Italy. The dominant feature of the *Rule* is its insistence on obedience. The monk must have no will of his own but must yield perfect obedience to the abbot of the monastery, who, on the other hand, must govern not arbitrarily but in accordance with the *Rule*. A second feature of the *Rule* is its moderate asceticism. Ample food, sleep, and other things necessary for the welfare of the body are provided for, and mortification of the flesh is discouraged; but all unnecessary luxuries are strictly forbidden. Another feature is an emphasis on manual labor—a revolutionary idea in a society which had considered this unworthy of freemen. The monk is to devote the greater part of his energy to manual labor, although provision is also made for intellectual labor, and formal religious services are to be held eight times a day. Still another feature is the doctrine that humility is the means by which the monk attains his goal. It is by mounting the twelve steps of humility that he will finally come to the love of God. The first step is that fear of God which makes one mindful of his commandments, and the last is having humility not only in the heart but even in outer appearance, with eyes always fixed on the ground.

The spirit of the *Rule* is shown by its prologue, which says:

We are about to institute a school for the service of God, in which we hope nothing harsh nor burdensome will be ordained. But if we proceed in certain things with some little severity, sound reason so advising for the amendment of vices or the preserving of charity, do not for fear of this forthwith flee from the way of salvation, which is always narrow in the beginning. In living our life, however, and by the growth of faith, when the heart has been enlarged, the path of God's commandments is run with unspeakable loving sweetness; so that never leaving his school, but persevering in the monastery until death in his teaching, we share by our patience in the sufferings of Christ, and so merit to be partakers of his kingdom.[2]

The Benedictine order, that is, the monasteries united by their observance of this *Rule,* although otherwise independent of each other, spread through western Europe, where it displaced other forms of monasticism, became a bulwark of civilization during the Dark Ages, and took a leading part in the Christianization of pagan nations. Its very success became its greatest danger. The labor of the monks, together with the donations of wealthy admirers, produced that material prosperity which it is the monk's vocation to renounce. The history of the order is a history of reforms resulting in prosperity which made new reform necessary. The Cluniac reform, one of the most influential, had its center in the monastery of Cluny in Burgundy, founded in 910 and dedicated to a strict observance of the *Rule*. The hundreds of Cluniac monasteries, with no abbots of their own but all governed by the one abbot of Cluny, were centers from which the monastic ideal of Christianity spread through the whole Church. But by the twelfth century even the Cluniacs were famous for art, scholarship, and magnificence rather than for renunciation or piety. The more popular and powerful monasticism became, the more it had to struggle against the temptation to forget its original purpose, which was to renounce the world in order to seek God.

## BERNARD OF CLAIRVAUX

The Cistercian reform began in 1098 when Robert, abbot of the monastery of Molesme in Burgundy, disgusted by the laxity of his own monks, retired with twenty of the more ascetic ones to the wilderness. Here they built the monastery of Citeaux and resolved to follow a literal interpretation of the *Rule*. Although Robert was compelled to return to Molesme, the others persevered at Citeaux. Under their English abbot Stephen Harding they persisted in their resolution, but for many years received no new members. As sickness reduced their numbers, the extinction of the monastery seemed imminent, when, one day in 1112, there was a knock at the gate. A group of thirty-two Burgundian noblemen sought to be admitted as novices. Their leader, a young man of twenty-two, was named Bernard.

This young nobleman wanted to become a Cistercian because he believed that only in a monastery, and in one which was so in fact as well as in name, would he be free to love the divine wisdom which is the Word of God. Called by his birth to a life of chivalry and by his talents to a career of scholarship, he had rejected both. Overcoming the temptations of the intellect by prayer and those of the flesh by such direct means as jumping into an icy pond, he had resolved to renounce the world. But he did not renounce those whom he loved, and would not seek his own salvation so long as they remained in peril. They must accompany him. Mothers hid their sons and wives their husbands at his approach—but in vain. Bernard's eloquence overwhelmed all. When the last one had yielded, he gathered his band of thirty-one relatives and friends and led them to Citeaux.

His three years there were the only years of his life which he spent as he wished—as an obscure monk. His example attracted so many others that it was soon necessary to found daughter monasteries, and Bernard, aged twenty-five, was named abbot of the third of these, Clairvaux. The administration of this monastery, which grew to have a population of nearly 700 persons, and the supervision of its sixty-eight daughters were tremendous tasks. But Bernard's influence extended far beyond his jurisdiction. Due to it the Cistercian family expanded during his lifetime from one monastery to 350 and established itself in all the countries of Latin Christendom. He encouraged reforms in the abbeys of Cluny and St. Denis which spread through the whole Benedictine order. He took an active part in the founding of the Templars and the Premonstratensians. By precept and example he set forth the monastic ideal; by eloquence and fervor he led men to embrace it.

Other works, which went beyond the proper duty of a monk, were forced upon him. The world which he had renounced would not renounce him. He refused five episcopal elections, but he could not refuse specific tasks to which he was summoned by princes or commanded by the pope. His arbitration was constantly sought in disputed elections and in controversies between church and state. More than once his intervention saved France or Germany from civil war. He stopped a massacre of Jews in Germany. He persuaded the emperor to renounce an attempt to reestablish the right of lay investiture. He led the long struggle which terminated the schism resulting from the election of two popes in 1130. Above all he appeared as a suppressor of heresies. He was one of the most outstanding men in Europe as he traveled from place to place, preceded by a reputation for sanctity and followed by reestablished peace. His influence seemed even to transcend the frontiers of Christendom when he became the protagonist of the second crusade. Everywhere men yielded to his preaching and took the cross. His eloquence was not in words alone; during his recruiting campaign in the Rhineland 172 blind men received their sight, 235 paralytics were restored to health. Converting the will of all by his eloquence, overcoming even physical evils by his miraculous cures, admitting his mystic communion with the eternal Word, he seemed like a great prophet. The news of the annihilation of the Christian army came like a flash of lightning from a clear sky. Denounced as the false prophet who had sent so many men to their death, humiliated in spirit by his first failure, broken in body by a disease which confined him to bed, he longed only for death, and soon attained it, in 1153.

The story of his inner life cannot be written, for Bernard did not compose any spiritual autobiography. But something can be learned from his writings. Bernard was a great master of Latin prose. The sweetness of his style, no less than that of his doctrine, has given him the title of Mellifluous Doctor. Thirteen essays, 336 sermons, and 454 letters are extant. His biographers reveal Bernard the prophet; his own writings reveal Bernard the mystic. Transient union with God in this life he attained; enduring union with God in the other life he longed for. After each of his many tasks he returned to the monastic seclusion which was his only delight, and this alternation of contemplative and active lives made possible the great influence he exerted. When he was on his deathbed, and his monks begged him to live for their sake, he answered that he was torn between two wishes—love for them urged him to stay, desire for Christ drew him to go. These words were an epitome of his whole life.

Although his writings are full of mystical doctrine, he never composed a systematic treatise on mysticism. His mystical philosophy, therefore, can only be learned by a comparative study of all his works. The next section will give a summary of his theory of freedom, as found in his only strictly philosophical book, a short essay called *Grace and Free Choice,* and the following section will give a systematic analysis of his mystical teachings.

## BERNARD'S THEORY OF FREEDOM

The problem of freedom has always been one of the most difficult problems of philosophy. In its metaphysical aspect the problem is: if all our acts are determined by some cause, how can we act freely? but if we freely choose what we will to do, how can our choice be governed by any cause? In its ethical aspect the problem is: if all our acts are determined by some cause, how can we be held responsible for them so as to be justly rewarded or punished? but if we are ourselves responsible for our free acts, how can they be determined by any chain of causes originating outside ourselves? In Christian theology the general problem assumes a special form. If we are saved by God's irresistible grace and inevitably damned when God withholds his grace, how is our salvation or damnation due to our own free acts? But if we are justly rewarded or punished in accordance with our own merits, how can this be due to the giving or withholding of a grace which is predetermined by God alone and completely beyond our control?

In the extensive and largely obscure literature on this problem, Bernard's lucid and penetrating little book *Grace and Free Choice* shines like a beacon. As a Christian theologian he discusses the problem of freedom in terms of grace, but his solution concerns the fundamental elements of the problem, and so is equally applicable to any other formulation of it, in which determinism is defined in terms of some other kind of causality. He does not choose between the alternatives, determinism and freedom, nor does he compromise by allotting to each a limited scope. We have, according to Bernard, both absolute determinism and absolute freedom.

Equal power or facility to choose either good or evil, that is, what we would call indeterminism, is not found anywhere, even in God. God, because of his steadfastness in the good, inevitably chooses the good. So do angels, while devils, because of their obstinacy in the evil, inevitably choose the evil. Man, naturally sinful, inevitably chooses evil when not aided by grace, but inevitably chooses good when he is so aided. Human indeterminism was lost irrecoverably at the fall. Man fell from the state of being able not to sin into the state of not being able not to sin, and is elevated by grace into the state of not being able to sin. The giving or withholding of grace, therefore, determines all choices which have moral significance. All our choices are, in modern terms, "theoretically predictable"—but the predictor would have to be sufficiently omniscient to fathom the causes of God's inscrutable grace.

Determinism does not imply lack of freedom. *Free* means *voluntary* or *willing*. The will is always free; to say it is not would be to say you will what you do not will, which is nonsense. Freedom means to do as you will. So long as you act as you will, you are acting freely, no matter what the efficient cause of your action may be. We are compelled to move unfreely, that is, unwillingly, when we are forcibly dragged from one place to another. But we cannot be compelled to *choose* unwillingly, because choosing implies willing that which is chosen. If we will two inconsistent acts, we choose the one we prefer, that is, will more. Since we always will what we choose, we always choose willingly, that is, freely, and so our choice is always free.

Men are distinguished from irrational animals by the possession of reason and will, which, together with the thinking faculty called memory, constitute the rational soul. The reason distinguishes; the will desires; together they consent. Reason and will together form the consenting faculty called free choice (*liberum arbitrium*). It is called free because it is willing and choice because it is rational. (It must not be translated "free will," because it is *liberum,* not *arbitrium,* which refers to the will.) The act of the reason is accompanied by the act of the will and therefore voluntary, that is, free. Since free choice is an intrinsic attribute of human nature, all men possess it absolutely (being with respect to this attribute equal to God) and under all conditions (except insanity, infancy, or sleep, in which they cease to be rational beings).

The possession of free choice does not imply that we cannot lack other kinds of freedom. The existence of misery shows that we are not able to enjoy what we will, and the existence of sin shows that we are not able to will what is good. To escape sin we need free counsel (*liberum consilium*), which is consent to the good, and to escape misery we need free enjoyment (*liberum complacitum*), which is delight in the good. These kinds of freedom are gifts of grace. The problem, therefore, is not so much how can we be free when subject to grace, as how can we be free even when not subject to grace. Both problems must be solved—the former to explain salvation, the latter to explain damnation. The solution of both is the same—we are free in either case because we always have free choice, that is, choose what we will.

We are morally responsible for what we do voluntarily. Merit pertains to the will. Free choice is justly capable of beatitude or misery because it is truly deserving of reward or punishment. Consent to the good, that is, voluntary choice of the good, is, because of the good will, meritorious and therefore deserving of reward. Consent to the evil is, because of the bad will, deserving of punishment. We are justly rewarded or punished for our choices because they are free in the sense of being voluntary, that is, accompanied by will. The efficient cause of the choice is irrelevant.

To be saved from sin is to consent to the good. Simply to consent, that is, to have free choice, is an intrinsic attribute of human nature. Without grace we consent to the evil, but not against our will, because it is free choice itself (reason and will) which consents. Grace compels free choice to consent to the good instead of the evil, and this consent is salvation. Thus we are compelled to be saved, but not against our will, because it is free choice itself which grace converts. Grace alone is the efficient cause of salvation. Free choice is the thing which is saved, that is, converted from free choice of evil to free choice of good. Without free choice there would be nothing to be saved, and without grace there would be nothing by which it is saved. Salvation, therefore, is wholly determined by God's predestined grace, and at the same time it is a perfectly free act of the soul. Since it is a free, that is, voluntary, act, it is deserving of reward, and so beatitude is given to the saved and withheld from the others with perfect justice.

## BERNARD'S MYSTICISM

His philosophy of mysticism can be learned only by a comparative study of his various works,[3] and such a study makes it possible to distinguish twelve steps in the path by which, according to Bernard, man can come to God. (This is an artificial systematization; he himself never made any such list of twelve steps.) The first step, or rather the base from which the path begins, is the sinful state of nature in which we find ourselves before we have received any grace beyond the grace of creation by which we are brought into being. Man was originally made in the image and likeness of God. The image of God, which is the rational soul, that is, the trinity of memory, reason, and will, is man's specific form, which cannot be lost. The likeness of God, which is the right functioning of these faculties in thinking, choosing, and willing the good, can be, and in fact has been, lost. Each of us, therefore, is created in the image, but not in the likeness, of God. Since we have free choice, which is capable of beatitude or misery, we are potentially blessed; but since we lack free counsel and free enjoyment, we are actually miserable.

The second step, which is the first step upward, is the fear of the Lord which is the beginning of wisdom. Love of God is the end of the anagogic path, but fear of God is its beginning. A man utterly depraved can be turned toward the good only by this motive. If he loves only the evil pleasures of the world he must hate the austerity of the Christian life, but if he hates the torments of hell even more he will embrace the Christian life as the lesser evil—not because he loves virtue but because he fears God's judgment. He flees from hell and hopes for heaven. This beginning of salvation is brought about by faith in the precepts, miracles, and promises of Christ. Moved by the promises and assured by the miracles, the believer observes the precepts.

This is that "first step of humility" described in the Benedictine *Rule*.

Taking the monastic vows is the third step. The man who fears God's wrath flees to a monastery as the only place in this wicked world where he can be reasonably safe. Here he learns asceticism, which is the renunciation of those physical vices which injure not only the soul but even the body itself, and obedience, which disciplines the will and leads it gradually to that absolute submission to God's will which makes contemplation possible. The monastic life has two purposes. Its more obvious purpose is to assure salvation by providing security against the temptations of the world. It is for this purpose that the sinner who fears God's judgment takes refuge in the monastery. But after he has persevered in the monastic life, he discovers its more profound purpose, which is to attain the vision of God, not merely to merit it. Men can acquire merit in the active life or in the scholastic life, although not so easily or certainly as in the monastic life, but they do not receive the reward of their merit. We believe that they will receive it in the next world. But monks are able not only to merit, but actually to attain in this world, the mystical contemplation of God which is man's highest good.

This joyful reward is not, of course, attained at the beginning of the monk's career, but at the end. The beginning is bitter suffering arising from the pangs of remorse as the humble monk recognizes his own sins. Humility is the fourth step. The whole *Rule* is designed for the development of humility, which means knowing yourself. The materialist who believes that he is not a rational soul made in God's image but a material animal like other animals, underestimates himself, and cannot possibly progress in wisdom. The proud man who exaggerates his own greatness by attributing the excellence he sees or imagines in himself not to God's grace but to his own exertion, overestimates himself, and will receive no further grace. The humble man recognizes his own glory, and at the same time recognizes that it is not his own. Reason alone is necessary—it may be against his will that a man sees his own littleness; and so humility is not a merit, for merit lies in good will. Humility is the first step of knowledge; it gives knowledge of truth in yourself.

Such purely rational humility might better be called humiliation in contrast with the voluntary and therefore meritorious humility to which it leads. The former is opposed to the pride which is blindness; the latter is opposed to the pride which is vanity. The former means knowledge of what it is to be a man; the latter means acceptance of the fact that you are a man and therefore willingness to undergo the toil and sorrow for which man is born. The former is consummated when you become, as a result of self-examination, perfectly contemptible in your own sight; the latter is consummated when you cannot endure to be other than contemptible in the sight of others.

Humility leads to charity. The psychological fact that humility leads us to love other people, while pride leads us to hate them, is the foundation on which the monastic community is based. The community is bound together by charity because each of its members is filled with humility. The first form of charity which humility produces is the active charity of good works, not the emotional passion of love. It is possible, at least at first, to do good to your neighbor without loving him, to do unto others as you would that they should do unto you not with the joyful freedom of a lover to whom nothing is more delightful than to serve his beloved, but sadly, as a grievous duty, because you ought to, not because you want to. This is the sixth step.

The seventh step is love. The subjective feeling of an emotion is the effect of its behavioristic expression. If you persistently act as if you loved somebody, you will eventually come really to love him. Active charity, therefore, even if begun as a disagreeable duty, finally develops into emotional love. Then the duty becomes a glad and free expression of the love within. Love is one of the four emotions (joy, sadness, fear, love) which we all have by nature. But in the state of nature we love only ourselves. Just as the superabundance of God's eternal self-love overflows into his love for his creatures, so our natural self-love, under the influence of humility and active charity, overflows into love of neighbor. Love of neighbor is fellow-feeling (*compassio, συμπάθεια*). It makes two persons to be one spirit, so that their wills become identical in object, although distinct in substance. The lover feels the beloved's joys and sorrows as his own. Becoming like his beloved, he acquires intuitive knowledge of his beloved, because intuition is based on likeness between subject and object. Love, therefore, is the second step of knowledge; it gives knowledge of truth in your neighbor. Love is the fulfillment of desire; the lover no longer desires the beloved object, because love implies that he already possesses it. "Love seeks no reason or fruit beyond itself. Its use is its fruit. I love because I love; I love in order to love." [4]

The eighth step is purity. "Desire for vanity is contempt of truth, and contempt of truth is the cause of our blindness." [5] When contempt of truth is replaced by humility and desire for vanity is replaced by love, reason and will are purified, and thus the soul is restored to that likeness of God in which man was originally made. Then, being like God, the soul is able to know God intuitively by contemplation.

When the monk has purified his soul by humility and love, if he then seeks, with strong desire, burning thirst, and constant meditation, to be united with the Word of God in mystical contemplation, he will surely succeed. He must first banish all sensations, sensuous desires, and sensory images, and even all human thoughts. The ineffable experience of God's presence is not phenomenal or conceptual, but emotional. "Contemplation is brought about by the condescension of the Word of God to human nature through grace and the exaltation of human nature to the Word through divine love." [6] God has a desire for the beauty of that soul which he observes to be walking in the spirit, especially if he sees it burning with love for him.

A soul thus loving and thus loved will not at all be satisfied, therefore, either with that manifestation of the bridegroom which is made to many through his creatures, or that which is made to few through visions and dreams, unless by a peculiar privilege it may also receive him coming down from heaven, in the love and very marrow of its heart, and may have its beloved in its presence, not perceived but absorbed, not appearing but affecting; and no doubt the more delightfully for being inward, not outward. [7]

Contemplation is not a confusion of two natures but an agreement of two wills. It is an agreement so perfect that the soul and God become one spirit. The soul which was God's slave through fear, God's hireling through humility, God's disciple through charity, and God's son through love, now becomes God's bride through contemplation. This is beatitude. The rational soul's beatitude consists of perfect understanding (the perfection of the reason), perfect joy (the perfection of the will), and perfect justice (the perfection of free choice). Contemplation gives perfect justice because it harmonizes the will with God's will, perfect joy as Bernard testifies from his own experience, and perfect understanding because it reveals eternal Truth. Contemplation is the third step of knowledge; it gives knowledge of Truth in itself. This beatitude is imperfect only because it is transient. Contemplation is interrupted by the requirements of the body, the sting of some care, the pang of some sin, above all by the flood of sensory images which rush into the mind. And even the perfect mystic is recalled, if by nothing else, by the requirements of fraternal charity.

These requirements lead to the tenth step, which is the mystic's return to the active life to preach the wisdom he has learned and to perform miracles of healing. Such works are the fecundity of the spiritual marriage, by which the soul bears spiritual offspring to its divine bridegroom, and the beatitude of one individual becomes a source of spiritual life in others.

The eleventh step is mounted when the soul is finally released from the corruptible body, so that contemplation is no longer interrupted by its necessities and desires. Although the ordinary saints in heaven have for their highest consolation the vision of the human Christ, the mystic has already during his earthly life attained to something higher than that, namely, contemplation of the divine Word. In heaven his contemplation is more perfect because it is constant. Although reason and will are perfected, the third faculty of the soul, memory, is not satisfied by earthly contemplation, which passes and cannot be retained. The enduring contemplation possible only in heaven adds to the perfect understanding, joy, and justice a fourth perfection, perfect security, which is the perfection of the memory; and so it completes the beatitude of the whole soul. Even so, it is still subject to distractions. The disembodied souls never cease to long for their bodies; and the saints devote themselves to miracles of charity even more fervently than when on earth. They are freed from misery but not from desire; they rest in peace but not in glory.

Even the beatitude of the whole soul is not the beatitude of the whole man, for man consists of soul and body. The final step will come, therefore, only at the resurrection. The beatitude of the body will be immortality, impassibility, lightness, and beauty. The beatitude of the soul will be contemplation of the Word, no longer transient or enduring, but eternal, and made perfect by the absence of any possible distraction. There will be no desire for the body, no desires of the body, and no need for works of charity. Desire and charity will be consummated in perfect love, and faith and understanding will be consummated in perfect vision. The saints will see God as he is, because they will be as he is.

## MYSTICISM AND MONASTICISM

Bernard was the most famous mystic of the twelfth century because of his eloquence and his activity as a reformer and statesman, not because of his mysticism, for there was nothing unique about that. It might almost be said that the only monks who were not mystics were those who failed to reach the goal of their vocation. Bernard distinguished three types of monks: those who, like himself, had attained to contemplation of the Word of God; those less proficient, unable to contemplate the Word, but able to contemplate the saints and angels in heaven; and those not yet capable of any contemplation. Mysticism and mystical writing flourished both in the Benedictine order and in new orders less strict or more strict than it.

Less strict than the Benedictines were the Regular Canons, who were something intermediate between monks and secular priests. They lived together under the monastic vows, but they were governed by the relatively liberal Augustinian Rule, and their vocation was to perform the ordinary duties of priests in the world. Their monastery of St. Victor at Paris, founded by William of Champeaux, became a center of mystical literature. Richard of St. Victor, one of these writers, in his essay on *The Four Steps of Passionate Love* (*De quatuor gradibus violentae charitatis*),[8] calls the four steps of love betrothal, marriage, copulation, and childbearing. On the first the soul is wounded by love, so that it burns with desire for God; on the second it is bound by love, unable to free itself even for a moment from the thought of God; on the third it is given up to love so exclusively that all other affections are expelled and all actions whatever are impossible; on the fourth it is never satisfied, but eager to do and suffer all things for God's sake. The first step is meditative desire, the second is contemplative exaltation, the third is joyous ecstasy, the fourth is compassionate action in serving other men. On the first the divinely inspired soul returns to itself; on the second it is lifted up to God; on the third it passes over into God; on the fourth it comes forth again to descend even below itself. Glorified on the third, it is humbled on the fourth; killed into God, it is resurrected into Christ.

More strict than the Benedictines, on the other hand, were the Carthusians, who were something intermediate between monks and hermits. They lived together in a monastery, but each in his own cell, where he mortified the flesh by a strict asceticism and devoted most of his time to solitary work and prayer. Guigo, prior of their parent monastery the Grande Chartreuse, and like Richard a contemporary of Bernard, sets forth the Carthusian ideal in his essay *The Ladder to Heaven* (*Scala paradisi*).[9] There are, he says, four steps of spiritual activity: reading, meditation, prayer, and contemplation. Reading seeks, meditation discovers, prayer demands, and contemplation tastes the sweetness of the blessed life. Reading is the careful and attentive perusal of the scriptures. Meditation is the mind's zealous action in searching out the knowledge of hidden truth by means of its own reason. Prayer is the heart's devoted application to God for removing what is evil and obtaining what is good. Contemplation is the elevation of the mind rapt into God as it tastes the joys of eternal delight. This path is more intellectual than that described by Bernard or Richard, although its final step is purely emotional, when contemplation "inebriates the thirsty soul with the dew of celestial sweetness." The solitary monk in his cell has little opportunity to exhibit love for others, even his fellow monks; and it is noteworthy that Bernard himself, in a letter written to the Carthusians, in telling how love leads us from humility to contemplation, speaks only of love of God, and not of love of neighbor, as when addressing his own Cistercians.

The tradition of the mystic's duty to return from his contemplation to help his unenlightened fellow creatures is at least as old as Plato's allegory of the cave. The difference in attitude toward the relation between contemplation and action is one of the most striking differences in the accounts of the mystical path given by Bernard, Richard, and Guigo. It is a difference which follows from the nature of the monastic orders to which they belonged. Guigo, a Carthusian, that is, a hermit, calls "the usefulness of honest action" one of the causes which interfere with contemplation. He admits that it, unlike other causes of interference, is "tolerable," but it is clear that he does not consider it desirable and that no Carthusian would deliberately seek an opportunity for action in the world. William of St. Thierry, writing to a Carthusian community, says bluntly, "To serve God is others' business, to cleave to him is yours." [10] Bernard, a Benedictine, that is, an ordinary monk, considers contemplation and action equally important, but the former the highest good for the soul itself, the latter merely a duty to others. The soul is compelled to action by its neighbors' necessity, but it is drawn to contemplation by the beauty of the Word. It interrupts its contemplation willingly in order to be useful, but it longs for the time when it will no longer have to. But Richard, a Regular Canon, that is, a priest, regards a mystic who does not express his contemplation in action as a barren wife. Such a one may enjoy union with God, but to no avail. The soul which has reached only the third step of love has not yet attained the fecundity which is the fruition and whole purpose of its love.

While these monastic philosophers of the twelfth century, who initiated the long line of medieval and modern mystics, differ so radically with regard to the practical application of mysticism, they agree fundamentally with regard to its philosophy. They all teach that beatitude is union with God, that this union is attained in ecstatic contemplation, that the nature of this contemplation is love, and that this love is made possible by a regulated life directed to that end. Besides the other two ways of seeking wisdom, that of faith based on authority and that of understanding based on reason, they teach a third way, that of intuition based on love.

# Chapter V. ISAAC OF STELLA

## SCHOLASTIC AND MONASTIC PHILOSOPHY

THERE are two kinds of philosophy, two ways of loving wisdom. For some philosophers the purpose of philosophy is to understand being more truly by right thinking. For others it is to participate in being more fully by right living. For the former philosophy is something to be learned. For the latter it is a way of life.

In the twelfth century both kinds of philosophy were equally popular. Lovers of theoretical wisdom crowded the schools where it was supposed to be taught, and lovers of practical wisdom crowded the monasteries where it was supposed to be practiced. Abelard and Bernard were outstanding examples and champions of the scholastic philosophy and the monastic philosophy, respectively.

## ISAAC OF STELLA

A remarkable synthesis of scholasticism and monasticism was effected by a Cistercian abbot who established his mysticism on a foundation of dialectic. Isaac's life demonstrated that a scholar need not be worldly nor a monk ignorant, and his doctrine demonstrated that the philosophical presuppositions of monastic practice are intelligible in terms of scholastic theory. The great monastic dilemma, the conflicting claims of personal salvation and charity for others, he solved by becoming a Benedictine, which implies acknowledging the equal validity of both claims. The great scholastic dilemma, realism versus nominalism, he solved by accepting both the extreme realist doctrine that individuals are nothing and the extreme nominalist doctrine that universals are nothing. He saw no incompatibility between them but simply deduced their logical consequence, which is that all creatures are nothing. This is just what Bernard had always maintained and given as the reason why the only true knowledge is the contemplation of that "being of himself and of all things" who alone truly is.

Isaac of Stella was born in England, became a monk at Citeaux, was chosen abbot of the Cistercian monastery of Stella near Poitiers, and died there about 1169. At one time he led a group of monks to establish a new monastery in the barren wilderness of the island of Re near La Rochelle, but this project had to be abandoned. At Stella, harassed by war, famine, and pestilence, he lived the life of an obscure abbot, withdrawn from the world, devoted to meditation and preaching.

His preaching, which was strongly impressed by the scholastic studies of his youth, was marked by such originality that his learned monks used to protest when they detected any lack of it. It was also marked by tolerance. He spoke with the greatest reverence of Bernard as an almost superhuman example of perfect charity. But unlike Bernard he defended the orthodoxy and morality of the scholastics, although criticizing them for giving possible future heretics a precedent for preferring novelty to authority.[1] And unlike Bernard, who in eulogizing the Templars declared that "a Christian glories in the death of a pagan," Isaac protested that massacring and plundering the infidels was not in accord with "Christ's meekness, patience, and way of preaching." [2]

His published works, written in a concise and graceful Latin, include fifty-four sermons and two essays, on *The Soul* and on *The Office of the Mass*. The next section will summarize the dialectical argument of a series of sermons on the parable of the sower,[3] preached during the difficult days on the island of Re, and the following two sections will describe the metaphysical and psychological doctrine of the essay on *The Soul*.[4] The contrast between the sermons and the essay, the former opposing the nothingness of creatures to the allness of God, the latter comparing the similarities and dissimilarities found in God and various kinds of creatures, shows how Isaac distinguished between the existential being according to which creatures are radically other than God and the essential nature according to which they are more or less the image of God.

## ONTOLOGY

All things which exist, exist either through themselves or not through themselves. If not through themselves, they exist through another to which they adhere in order to exist, and are called adherents or accidents. If through themselves, they are called substances. For example, Man exists through himself, and any particular man exists through himself, but his wisdom or folly, tallness or shortness, whiteness or blackness exist not through themselves but through him. It is the property of accidents, which include the nine other categories, to adhere to substances, and it is the property of substances to be susceptible of contrary accidents and therefore mutable. All substances exist through themselves, but they may exist in either of two ways. They may, like Man, exist only abstractly in nature and the reason and the understanding; or they may, like any particular man, exist both in nature and in act, both in reason and in reality, both in understanding and in status. The latter are numerically one both in reason and in reality, and are substances in the strict sense; they are called first substances. The former are suspended in the understanding and conceived confusedly by the mind as common to many particulars; they are called second substances. First substances exist in themselves, but second substances exist only in the first substances which exist in reality. Any particular man exists in himself, but Man exists only in the various men, and if there were no men, Man would exist nowhere and so would not be at all. Second substances exist of themselves, but first substances exist only of the second substances which preexist in reason. Man exists of himself, requiring for his existence nothing but the differentiated genus mortal rational animal, but a particular man exists only of Man, and if there were no such thing as Man there could be no particular men exemplifying it. All things, therefore, are imperfect—accidents do not exist through themselves, second substances do not exist in themselves, first substances do not exist of themselves. All things are dependent on something else for their being and therefore, considered alone by themselves, are not. Accidents are the forms by which generic second substances are differentiated into specific second substances and by which specific second substances are exemplified in first substances. Accidents are nothing apart from the second substances of which they are determinations. Second substances are nothing apart from the first substances in which they are posited. First substances are nothing apart from the accidents by which they are differentiated. All separate things are nothing, and therefore all combinations are nothing, for a combination of two nothings can produce only nothing. All creatures composed of matter and form are nothing, because matter is mere substance, which is nothing, and form is mere accident, which is nothing. *If a man think himself to be something, when he is nothing, he deceiveth himself.* If God can say *I am who am,* all others must confess, I am who am not.[5]

That which is most worthy and than which nothing can be better, must exist through itself, of itself, and in itself. It must be immutable, for it is obvious that the immutable is better than the mutable, and this is confirmed by the authority of the apostle: *with whom is no variableness, neither shadow of turn-*

*ing.* Being immutable, it is simple and one. One, it transcends all second substances, for unity is the principle of all things. Simple, it transcends all first substances, which are compounded of matter and form. Immutable, it transcends all substance whatever, corporeal or incorporeal, for mutability is the property of substance.[6] It is not any of all things; still less is it nothing at all; neither is it, like Plato's matter, intermediate between something and nothing. One before all things, simple after all things, immutable above all things—it is the creator, sustainer, and ruler of the universe. This supersubstance alone truly is, since all else has been shown to be nothing. Being better than any substance, it alone deserves to be worshiped, even if it does not exist, since it can at least be thought.

Its existence, however, is demonstrable. The atheist, if he concedes his own existence, must admit that his own first cause is either himself or something else—in the latter case he acknowledges God's existence; in the former he is himself God. If anything exists, the one simple immutable cause of all diversity and composition and motion must exist. The eternal existence of truth itself, which the atheist must concede if he claims his own doctrine to be eternally true, proves the existence of the immutable—unless something mutable and consequently temporal has existed from eternity, which is absurd. These proofs are based not on verbal inference but on the nature of God. If anything exists, the first cause of all things must exist. Even if no thing exists (as was in fact the case before the creation), still he exists who can bring into existence everything which either is or can be.[7]

Having found that God is and what he is not, we must inquire what he is. This is not absolutely impossible. God is ineffable —intrinsically so, not merely through the weakness of our understanding. But something can be affirmed truly, although not accurately, even of the ineffable. Divine theology, which describes

God literally, can affirm nothing of him, but denies all attributes to him. Symbolic theology, which describes God metaphorically, calls him a lion, a bird, etc. Between the two is rational theology, which describes God neither literally nor metaphorically but by understatement. God is truly wise and just—but not in the same way that a man is wise or just; and to call him wise or just is to fall short of the truth.

God's simplicity means that he is whatever he has. Since he is that than which nothing better can be, he is obviously wise and just, that is, has wisdom and justice, and consequently is wisdom and justice. This is absurd, because he is not anything, yet it is true in the sense of understatement. Just as he is called super-substance, so he can be called superwisdom and superjustice, and similarly of other attributes. This means that he is the source of wisdom and of justice and of all things—not as one thing is the source of another of the same nature (as the spring is the source of the river), but as the efficient cause, like an artisan, whose nature is different from that of the artifact he makes. But this too is an understatement, because the artisan only makes artifacts which are of the same nature as his raw material, whereas God creates things from nothing, annihilates things into nothing, changes one sort of thing into another, increases without adding, and decreases without taking away. He is no thing, but the efficient cause of all things; truly existing in himself, yet giving to other things a different sort of existence. As unity, he is not any number, but is the efficient cause of all numbers—for example, two is merely twice unity (not two unities, for there is only one), and so in two nothing but unity truly exists. As simplicity, he is the efficient cause of all compounds. As immutability, he is the efficient cause of all motion. He is the essence of all things—not that mutable essence by reason of which they are truly nothing, but the immutable essence by which all things are truth and life together once and forever, the source and efficient cause of essence, wisdom, justice, and all things—having them and being them not as they are in things but whence they are in things. Through the good and beautiful things which are made the understanding tries to discern that best and most beautiful by which they are made.[8]

In God we must distinguish what he is from what he has—not in denotation, for they are identical, but with regard to his being and his having, respectively. What he is has what he has. The latter, therefore, is of the former, while the former is not of anything. Hence the latter is called the offspring, or (as we usually say) the Son, of the former; while the former is, to continue the metaphor, called the Father of the latter. Rational theology distinguishes, therefore, between God as wisdom and God as wisdom of wisdom, between God as justice and God as justice of justice, etc. The relation between Father and Son is ineffable. Just as there is no noun to describe what God is, so there is no verb to describe what God does—for one reason because none of the tenses of our grammar refers to eternal action. Resorting to understatement and choosing the most nearly suitable verb from human psychology, we say that God speaks—but with the reservations that it is not speaking and is not in the present tense. The human soul has three faculties: memory, reason, and inventiveness—directed to the past, present, and future, respectively. Inventiveness searches out unknown things. Reason judges things found by inventiveness or regurgitated by memory, speaking them either audibly in the mouth of the body or by meditation in the mouth of the heart. Memory stores away things judged by reason and regurgitates them to be judged again. In God there is nothing corresponding to memory or inventiveness, for he has nothing past or future. Everything which he has, he has simultaneously present, or rather supersimultaneously superpresent in eternity. Everything which he has, therefore, he is eternally speaking, and so what he has is called his Word.[9] In it all things exist actually, that is by eternally present prescience, but also potentially, for it is the source, that is the exemplar, of all things which are or can be. All things exist in the immutable exemplar, where they are truth and life, more truly than in the substantial example, where they are mutable and unreal. The creation, by which sensible things are made, does not, therefore, bring anything into being, for all created things existed even more truly before their creation, together with the infinity of things never yet created.

It remains to inquire why there should have been a creation at all, why that which is infinite wills to supplement itself by that which is nothing, and especially why Plato says God rejoiced with great joy and Genesis says he saw everything to be very good, after creating the world, when he could find greater clarity of vision, greater goodness, and greater occasion for rejoicing within himself. The solution is to be found in this very interior rejoicing itself. If what God is rejoices in, and loves, what God has, this joy or love must be identical with God, because of his simplicity, and yet it is neither Father nor Son, because it proceeds from both, and so it is a third element, which we call the Holy Ghost. God is light (to make an understatement). A light gives light by shining, and these three things—to be a light, to shine, and to give light—are identical, yet distinguishable. The light which is given comes from the light which shines and from its shining; the shining comes from the light which shines; the light which shines has no source but itself. But it is the nature of light to be visible. The light which shines is visible through its shining because it gives light. Light is precious just because it is visible—that is, giveable, receivable, and enjoyable. Its whole use lies in its gift, that is, the light which is given.[10] This is true whatever understatement we employ. Whether we call the Holy Ghost light, goodness, joy, or love; its nature is to be giveable, receivable, and enjoyable, and to share itself with others. God therefore wills to be enjoyed—not through any necessity or desire, but through the very nature of his intrinsic goodness and joy, which is to extend itself to others, that they may share in that goodness and joy. Compelled by his own goodness and joy, a compulsion which is the highest freedom, he created the rational soul capable of enjoying him. He made it rational in order to search him out in itself and in all things, concupiscible in order to love and desire him, irascible in order to reject all things opposing this contemplation and delight; and he created the corporeal world for its service. The highest good of the rational soul is to do that for which it is made, namely, to enjoy God by contemplation, to see the light which shines by the light which it gives.[11]

## COSMOLOGY

The various sorts of beings form a "golden chain," in which each link differs only slightly from the next one, of which it is an image, and to which it is joined by likeness. One extremity is God, absolutely simple; the other is body, absolutely composite. The chain includes beings which are purely incorporeal, truly incorporeal, almost incorporeal, almost corporeal, and corporeal.

1. God is *purely incorporeal* because he is absolutely simple. He has neither quality nor quantity, that is, neither attributes distinct from himself nor quantitative parts. He *is* everything which he *has;* that is, he is identical with all his attributes, and has no accidents. Being of and for himself, he is in every way self-sufficient, and needs no body, place, time, cause, or form in order to exist. He is in himself—and consequently where he was before he made the world and would be should it cease to exist. Being infinite, he

is everywhere, and the whole of God is in each creature. Himself invisible, he is seen in and through every creature by those who have eyes to see.

2. The created spirit is *truly incorporeal* because it is simple, yet not purely incorporeal because it is also composite. It has quality but not quantity. In part it *is* what it *has;* that is, it is identical with its natural attributes, which include its faculties or powers. It has no quantitative parts, because its faculties, although distinct in property and operation, are not distinct in essence; they are not each a spirit but are all one spirit. But in part it *is not* what it *has;* that is, it is not identical with its accidental attributes, which include the acts of its powers, which are gifts, and which by habit may become virtues. The spirit's natural faculties, such as rationality, cannot be abstracted from it, but its accidental virtues, such as justice, can be abstracted and considered in their own essence, which is God. Like God the created spirit needs no body and therefore no place in order to exist, but unlike God it is mutable and therefore in time.

There are two kinds of created spirit, the angel and the human soul, the same in nature but different in condition. The angel does not ordinarily unite with body, but the soul, although nowise needing a body in order to exist, unites with a living body to use as an instrument. Being spiritual and so placeless, the soul is not in the body spatially, but takes it as an instrument to use and enjoy. Itself invisible, it is seen in and through its body. Just as the whole of God is in each creature, so the whole indivisible soul is in each member of the body (although not in the strict sense in which God is in each creature because in himself). But unlike God the soul is finite and limited, not in place but in powers and faculties, and consequently is manifested through one body only, so that, in the sense in which it is said to be there, it is said not to be elsewhere. The soul's withdrawal from the body is the effect, not the cause, of the body's death. It does not withdraw voluntarily, but when the body, as a result of bodily causes, dies, that is, becomes so disorganized as to be incapable of containing a soul, the soul reluctantly withdraws with all its faculties, that is, ceases to be manifested there. Its withdrawal does not affect its existence, essence, or place. The spiritual soul continues to exist unchanged after the death of the body, just as a melody continues to exist after the destruction of the musical instrument through which it was manifested, or a meaning after the cessation of the words by which it was expressed, or a number after the disappearance of the things counted.

3. The incorporeal forms of corporeal things are *almost incorporeal* because, although needing body, and consequently both time and place, in order to exist, they are themselves neither body nor likeness of body. They include the natures of bodies, which are second substances, and the dimensions and other properties of bodies, which are accidents. They are not separated from their bodies in actuality, but they are abstracted from them in consideration and studied by mathematics. Like spirits they are incorporeal, but unlike spirits they exist actually only in particular bodies, and so in place and time.

4. Likenesses of bodies are *almost corporeal* because, although not actually bodies, they are like bodies. They are images, unreal forms of corporeal things, existing apart from any real things. Like the incorporeal forms of bodies they are not real bodies, but unlike them they cannot be abstracted from time or place.

5. Body is *corporeal* because it is absolutely composite. It has both quality and quantity. It *is not* anything which it *has;* that is, it is not identical either with its natural attributes or with its accidents. It has quantitative parts, each of which is itself a body. Like images bodies exist in time and place, but unlike images they are external and real.

There are five kinds of body: fire or light, the subtlest, which is most like the "almost incorporeal," and which occupies the loftiest place in the physical cosmos, the highest heaven or empyrean; subtle air or ether, which forms the firmament; dense air or vapor; water; and earth, the densest and lowest.

The animal body, including the human, is completely corporeal, and needs no soul in order to live. Its highest part, composed mostly of fire, is its sensuality, the so-called "bodily spirit," which, although purely corporeal and nowise spiritual, is able to discern, choose, and reject just like a true spirit. The human body is so harmoniously organized that it is adapted to contain a soul, as a musical instrument is adapted to contain a melody. The corporeal body and the incorporeal soul are joined in personal union without confusion of natures. Their union, which takes place in the head, is brought about by the likeness between the body's highest part, its sensuality, and the soul's lowest part, its "phantasy" or power of sense-perception, which, being a fire-like force, easily unites with the fiery sensuality in accordance with the law that like coheres with like.

## PSYCHOLOGY

The soul, intermediate between God and body, through its lowest part coheres with body and through its highest part coheres with God. Its faculties, diverse in property, are identical with itself—the soul's life, sentience, or will are simply the soul living, sentient, or willing. Its faculties are powers receptive of gifts, vessels created empty but capable of being filled. Burdened by sin and by the corruptible body, these powers remain for the most part potential only. While the soul has the faculties and instruments of knowing and loving by nature, it can have knowledge of truth and order of love only from grace. All men have the same faculties, but different men have different gifts, and perhaps only in Jesus have the human faculties been filled to their utmost capacity.

By rationality the soul is capable of being illumined for knowing something; by concupiscence and irascibility it is capable of being affected for loving or hating something. Love gives rise to joy and hope; hate, to grief and fear; and these four emotions are the elements of which all virtues and vices are composed. Sentience, arising from rationality, is distinguished according to time as reason, memory, and inventiveness, or according to its object as bodily sense, imagination, reason, intellect, and intelligence. Knowing the five kinds of beings by these five faculties, the soul is said to be "the likeness of all things," and corresponding to the "golden chain" descending from God down to earth is the "upright ladder" ascending from touch up to intelligence.

Body is known by *bodily sense*—so called because its objects and instruments are corporeal, although, as a faculty of the soul, it is itself purely spiritual. As the one uniform mass of water in a vessel forms variously shaped streams as it flows out through variously shaped holes, so the one uniform sense or "phantasy" which is the soul's lowest faculty, together with the one uniform sensuality which is the body's highest activity, acts variously through various organs to perceive various kinds of body. By touch throughout the primarily earthy human body, by taste through the palate, by smell through the nose, by hearing through the ears, and by vision through the fiery eyes, the soul perceives earth, water, vapor, ether, and light, respectively. The spiritual faculty and the bodily organ, however, are not sufficient to produce perception. An aid from *without* must be given. In order to have vision, for example, the external light which is to be seen must, by shining, give light to the eye.

Likenesses of bodies are known by *imagination,* which perceives corporeal forms of corporeal things in time and space but apart from any real bodies. The necessary aid comes not from without but from *below,* that is, from the soul's phantasy, already filled with the phantasms created by bodily sense. These phantasms, once created, are able to rise into the imagination even when the corresponding external body is no longer present. They may be thus evoked either through the soul itself or through the operation of some other spirit either good or bad. In these images the soul, whether awake or asleep, temporarily deprived of senses or completely overcome, seems to itself to be doing or suffering something. Imagination has the same varieties as bodily sense.

The incorporeal forms of corporeal things are known by *reason,* which abstracts from bodies the second substances and accidents which exist in bodies. It abstracts them not in action but in consideration, and while it sees that they subsist actually only in body, it none the less perceives that they are not body. Unlike sense, which must be given aid from without the soul, or imagination, which must be given aid from a lower faculty of the soul, reason is aided from *within.* It has from its own nature (that is, by creating grace, by which all men are illumined) the illumination which permits it to know its proper objects.

The created spirit is known by *intellect,* the faculty by which the soul knows directly the incorporeal forms of incorporeal things, that is, itself, other souls, and angels. But since the created spirit is the likeness of God, and whoever can know either of two similar objects can know both, the soul when it lost the knowledge of God likewise lost the knowledge of itself and other spirits. The curious soul in its lustful body has its sense and imagination so clouded that they see obscurely, its reason so clouded that it barely sees, its intellect and intelligence so clouded that they see almost nothing. Such a soul does not even know itself. Angels who wish to show themselves to a man cannot do so unless his intellect has been enlightened, but must show themselves to his imagination through bodily likenesses or to his sense through an assumed body. The faculty of intellect remains in us all, but in order to see it must be aided from *above* by a special gift of illuminating grace.

God is known by *intelligence*. Like intellect, this faculty must be aided by grace, that is, from *above;* theophanies descend into intelligence as phantasms ascend into imagination. But as in the case of sense, the illumination comes directly from the object itself. Just as the eye sees the sun only in the sunlight, so the intelligence sees the true divine light only in its light. Just as the intrinsic heat of a fire gives heat, and the intrinsic light of a light gives light, to bodies which approach them, and thus create in these bodies an accidental heat or light which they do not have from their own nature, so the essential wisdom and justice of the divine nature give themselves to spirits which approach them, and create in their intelligence an accidental wisdom and justice by which they participate in God.

Just as, although the eye of the flesh has from nature the faculty of seeing, and the ear that of hearing, the eye never attains vision through itself, or the ear hearing, without the aid of the outer light or sound; so also the rational spirit, being by the gift of creation capable of knowing the true and loving the good, never attains the actuality of wisdom or charity except when flooded with the radiance and inflamed with the heat of the inner light." [12]

As the soul, through its lowest faculty, sense, coheres with the highest aspect of body, sensuality, and thereby is united with a body; so the soul, through its highest faculty, intelligence, coheres with the nearest person of God, the Holy Ghost, God's gift, and thereby is united with God. Through the Holy Ghost, the light which is given, it knows the Word, the shining light, and through it the Father, the light which shines.

## LOVE AND TRUTH

Isaac's scholastic subtleties were a justification for his monastic discipline. The purpose of his ontological doctrine was to show his monks why they should seek knowledge of God; that of his psychological doctrine was to show them how they should seek it. Because the soul is relatively simple it must transcend those faculties by which it knows the composite things of the world—bodies, images, or ideas—in order to know itself or other spirits. Because the supersubstantial essence of all things is absolutely simple the soul must transcend even the faculty by which it knows itself in order to know this essence by cohering with it. It is by the way of the Beatitudes that the soul purifies itself from the lower forms of knowledge in order finally to give itself up to that supreme knowledge which comes only through intelligence. It must first be purified for virtue, then for truth; first for loving, then for seeing; first purged of the vices of perverse love and disordered emotion, then purged of the sensations, images, and thoughts of mutable things. Truth is the goal, but love is the way. *Charitate itur, veritate statur.* The pure in heart see God, and only those whose hearts are purified by love can have the knowledge of God which is man's eternal life. But since *charity never faileth,* love does not cease when it arrives at truth, but life is lived blessed and eternal in the truth of love and in the love of truth.[13] In showing that this love of wisdom is the common goal of the monk's life and the scholar's dialectic, Isaac's doctrine fused the mystical and the intellectual strains in early medieval philosophy.

# CONCLUSION

WHEN the twelfth-century statesman, scholar, and humanist John of Salisbury stated, in his great work on political theory the *Polycraticus,* "A philosopher is a lover of God," [1] he gave a definition which all the philosophers considered in this book would have accepted. To all of them the love of wisdom meant the love of God, and the practice of philosophy meant the life which expresses that love in the highest way of which human nature is capable. But they differed greatly in their understanding of what that way is.

According to Erigena, the philosopher is participating in a cosmic process. In turning from science, the empirical study of particular things, to wisdom, the rational investigation of their ideal causes existing eternally in the Word of God, he unites things with their causes in his thought. In resolving his own nature into the intellect which is its essence, he fulfills his own highest destiny, which for him as for all creatures is to return to the source whence he came.

For Anselm philosophy means a refusal to be satisfied with blind faith in revealed dogma, which may be sufficient for salvation but is not sufficient to meet the rational soul's desire for understanding. To understand God by reason alone is the philosopher's way of loving him. The great champion of rationalism, by insisting that all knowledge must be demonstrable, laid down a challenge which has influenced philosophic thought ever since.

For Abelard philosophy, logic, and Christianity are synonymous, all meaning the love of the Wisdom or Logos incarnate in Christ. But the philosopher has a special function, to defend the truth, that is, the faith on which our love of God depends, against the fallacious arguments of pseudo-philosophers, just as Plato, the greatest of philosophers, defended it against the attacks of the sophists. The weapon which he uses is the same which Plato used, dialectic, and so the study of dialectic is the necessary foundation of philosophy.

For Bernard the love of God is a conscious experience, man's highest good, not something merely to be hoped for in a future life but something to be enjoyed in this life. Dialectic does not give it. Bernard follows Paul instead of Plato when he declares, in criticism of the scholastics, "This is my higher philosophy, to know Jesus and him crucified." [2] The true philosophic life is the religious life of the monastery, in which the spiritual vision is purified by humility, which gives knowledge of truth in ourselves, love, which gives knowledge of truth in others, and contemplation, which gives knowledge of Truth in itself.

The broad-minded abbot Isaac, at once scholastic and Cistercian, agreed fundamentally with Bernard, but saw no opposition between mysticism and logic. His intellect demanded satisfaction no less than his love, and his dialectical analyses of God and the soul were the finest fruit of his religious life.

They had much in common. They held the same faith, spoke the same language, and read the same books. All exemplified the Platonic definition of a philosopher, given by Socrates in the *Phaedo,* as one who withdraws from a concern for temporal things in order to contemplate eternal truths, so far as is possible in this life, and looks forward to doing so more fully in the next life. But in personality, in method, and in interests they were very unlike. This unlikeness is an indication of the vastness of their common field, philosophy, with its many points of view and its many problems. Each contributed in his own way to the rich and varied pattern of the intellectual life of the period. Each gave a profound solution to one of the persistent problems of philosophy—the problem of nature, the problem of knowledge, the problem of universals, the problem of the anagogic path, and the problem of being. When they undertook to describe in words the ineffable nature of the supreme reality, Erigena called it the superbeing which is the being of all things; Anselm, that than which nothing greater can be thought; Abelard, a trinity of power, wisdom, and goodness; Bernard, the bridegroom of the soul; Isaac, that which exists through, of, and in itself. For diversity of philosophic interest, as well as for profundity of philosophic thought and brilliance in its literary expression, the early Middle Ages have a high place in the history of philosophy.

# NOTES

## I. JOHN SCOTUS ERIGENA

1. Migne, *Pat. Lat.*, CXXII, 511B.
2. *Ibid.*, 513B.
3. *Ibid.*, 814A.
4. *Ibid.*, 548D.
5. *Ibid.*, 1022C.
6. *Ibid.*, 509A.
7. *Ibid.*, 357D.
8. *Ibid.*, 516C.
9. *Ibid.*, 499B.
10. *Ibid.*, 724A.
11. *Ibid.*, 441A, 443A.
12. *Ibid.*, 444C.
13. *Ibid.*, 444Df.
14. *Ibid.*, 441B.
15. *Ibid.*, 472B.
16. *Ibid.*, 526A.
17. *Ibid.*, 866C.
18. *Ibid.*, 869Af.
19. *Ibid.*, 632C.
20. *Ibid.*, 516A.
21. *Ibid.*, 888C.
22. *Ibid.*, 452C.
23. *Ibid.*, 447C.
24. *Ibid.*, 589B.
25. *Ibid.*, 591D.
26. *Ibid.*, 459D.
27. *Ibid.*, 443B, 1046C.
28. *Ibid.*, 487B.
29. *Ibid.*, 455C.
30. *Ibid.*, 490B.
31. *Ibid.*, 451C.
32. *Ibid.*, 881B.
33. *Ibid.*, 553D.
34. *Ibid.*, 639B.
35. *Ibid.*, 559A.
36. *Ibid.*, 670C, 956C, 966C.
37. *Ibid.*, 615D.
38. *Ibid.*, 622C.
39. *Ibid.*, 494A.
40. *Ibid.*, 768B.
41. *Ibid.*, 552B.
42. *Ibid.*, 624A.
43. *Ibid.*, 547B.
44. *Ibid.*, 628D.
45. *Ibid.*, 552A.
46. *Ibid.*, 529A.
47. *Ibid.*, 563D.
48. *Ibid.*, 867A.
49. *Ibid.*, 501B.
50. *Ibid.*, 701D.
51. *Ibid.*, 701A.
52. *Ibid.*, 1019C.
53. *Ibid.*, 665A.
54. *Ibid.*, 560B.
55. *Ibid.*, 621D.
56. *Ibid.*, 636D.
57. *Ibid.*, 686A.

58. *Ibid.* 680D.

59. *Ibid.*, 633A, 640C, 678B.

60. *Ibid.*, 704C.

61. *Ibid.*, 528B.

62. *Ibid.*, 454A.

63. *Ibid.*, 454C.

64. *Ibid.*, 683A.

65. *Ibid.*, 824D.

66. *Ibid.*, 629A.

67. *Ibid.*, 800B.

68. *Ibid.*, 755B.

69. *Ibid.*, 475B.

70. *Ibid.*, 780B.

71. *Ibid.*, 779B.

72. *Ibid.*, 571C.

73. *Ibid.*, 843A.

74. *Ibid.*, 966D.

75. *Ibid.*, 976A.

76. *Ibid.*, 863B.

77. *Ibid.*, 848C.

78. *Ibid.*, 583B.

79. *Ibid.*, 799B.

80. *Ibid.*, 536C.

81. *Ibid.*, 952C.

82. *Ibid.*, 989D.

83. *Ibid.*, 892D.

84. *Ibid.*, 451B.

85. *Ibid.*, 451D.

86. *Ibid.*, 1019B.

87. *Ibid.*, 627C.

88. *Ibid.*, 519B.

89. *Ibid.*, 536C.

90. *Ibid.*, 836C.

91. *Ibid.*, 1020B.

92. *Ibid.*, 876A.

93. *Ibid.*, 912A.

94. *Ibid.*, 993A.

95. *Ibid.*, 913B.

96. *Ibid.*, 979A.

97. *Ibid.*, 906B.

98. *Ibid.*, 943D.

99. *Ibid.*, 1020D.

100. *Ibid.*, 451B.

## II. ANSELM OF CANTERBURY

1. *Monologion*, Preface.

2. *Cur Deus homo*, I, i.

3. *De fide Trinitatis*, ii.

4. *Proslogion*, i.

5. *Ibid.*, ii.

6. Aquinas, *Summa Theol.*, I, 2, 1, ad 2. Cf. Daniels, A., *Quellenbeiträge und Untersuchungen zur Geschichte der Gottesbeweise im dreizehnten Jahrhundert mit besonderer Berücksichtigung des Arguments im Proslogion des hl. Anselm* (*Beiträge zur Geschichte der Philosophie und Theologie des Mittelalters*, VIII, 1–2).

7. Descartes, *Meditationes de prima philosophia*, V.

8. Kant, *Critique of Pure Reason,* Trans. Dial., II, iii, 5 (Müller's trans.).

9. Hegel, *History of Philosophy,* II, ii, B, 1, a (Haldane and Simson's trans.).

## III. PETER ABELARD

1. Cousin, *Ouvrages inédits d'Abélard,* p. 522.

2. Anselmus, *De fide Trinitatis,* ii.

3. Cousin, *Ouvrages inédits d'Abélard,* p. c.

4. *Ibid.,* p. 513; Geyer (ed.), *Logica "Ingredientibus"* (*Beiträge zur Geschichte der Philosophie und Theologie des Mittelalters,* XXI, 1), p. 10.

5. *Historia calamitatum,* ii; Cousin, *Ouvrages inédits d'Abélard,* p. 518; *Logica "Ingredientibus,"* p. 14; Lefèvre, G., *Les variations de Guillaume de Champeaux et la question des universaux* (*Travaux et mémoires de l'Université de Lille,* VI, 20), p. 25.

6. Cousin, *Ouvrages inédits d'Abélard,* pp. 524–541.

7. *Logica "Ingredientibus,"* pp. 9–16.

8. *Ibid.,* pp. 16–24.

9. Ostlender (ed.), *Theologia "Summi boni"* (*Beiträge zur Geschichte der Philosophie und Theologie des Mittelalters,* XXXV, 2–3), p. 36; *Theologia Christiana,* ed. Cousin (*Petri Abaelardi opera,* Vol. II) p. 463, *Pat. Lat.* CLXXVIII 1227C; *Introductio ad theologiam,* ed. Cousin (*Petri Abaelardi opera,* Vol. II) p. 67, PL 1040A.

10. Epist. 13, ed. Cousin (*Petri Abaelardi opera,* Vol. I) p. 698, PL 355C.

11. *Theol. S. b.,* p. 4; *Theol. Christ.,* ed. Cousin p. 361, PL 1126C; *Int. ad theol.,* ed. Cousin p. 22, PL 998B.

12. *Theol. S. b.,* p. 3; *Theol. Christ.,* ed. Cousin p. 359, PL 1124A; *Int. ad theol.,* ed. Cousin p. 13, PL 989C.

13. *Theol. S. b.,* p. 54; *Theol. Christ.,* ed. Cousin p. 484, PL 1247D; *Int. ad theol.,* ed. Cousin p. 93, PL 1065A.

14. Substituted for Abelard's example, *ensis* and *mucro,* which is not easily translated.

15. *Theol. S. b.*, p. 61; *Theol. Christ.*, ed. Cousin p. 490, PL 1253D; *Int. ad theol.*, ed. Cousin p. 95, PL 1067A.
16. Bernardus, Epist. 330, 332, 336; *De erroribus Abaelardi*, iv, 9.
17. Bernardus, *De consideratione*, V, iii, 6.
18. *Int. ad theol.*, ed. Cousin p. 5, PL 981C.
19. *Ibid.*, ed. Cousin pp. 3, 115; PL 980A, 1085C.
20. *Ibid.*, ed. Cousin p. 90, PL 1061D (cf. Augustinus, *De Trinitate*, VII, v, 10).
21. Bernardus, *De consideratione*, V, vi, 13.
22. Bernardus, *In Cantica*, Sermo 4, 4.
23. *Scito teipsum*, ed. Cousin (*Petri Abaelardi opera*, Vol. II) p. 603, PL 642D.
24. Bernardus, *De diversis*, Sermo 6, 1.


## IV. BERNARD OF CLAIRVAUX

1. This definition is adapted from Gasquet's introduction to his translation of the Benedictine *Rule* (London, 1909).
2. Benedictus, *Rule*, Prologue (Gasquet's trans.).
3. See the references at the end of the Preface. For fuller references see Bernard, *Steps of Humility* (Cambridge, Mass., 1940), pp. 49–112.
4. *In Cantica*, Sermo 83, 4.
5. Epist. 18, 1.
6. *De diversis*, Sermo 87, 3.
7. *In Cantica*, Sermo 31, 6.
8. Migne, *Pat. Lat.*, CXCVI, 1207–1224.
9. *Ibid.*, XL, 997–1004.
10. *Ibid.*, CLXXXIV, 311C.


## V. ISAAC OF STELLA

1. Migne, *Pat. Lat.*, CXCIV, 1853D.
2. *Ibid.*, 1854C.
3. *Ibid.*, 1749D–1777D.

4. *Ibid.*, 1875B–1890A.
5. Sermo 19.
6. Sermo 20.
7. Sermo 21.
8. Sermo 22.
9. Sermo 23.
10. Sermo 24.
11. Sermo 25.
12. Migne, *Pat. Lat.*, CXCIV, 1887D.
13. *Ibid.*, 1744B.

## CONCLUSION

1. Migne, *Pat. Lat.*, CXCIX, 652B.
2. Bernardus, *In Cantica,* Sermo 43, 4 (1 Cor. 2.2).

# BIBLIOGRAPHY

## GENERAL REFERENCE WORKS ON
## EARLY MEDIEVAL PHILOSOPHY

Migne, J. P. (editor). Patrologiae cursus completus, series Latina. Paris, 1844–1864. 221 volumes, of which the last four are indices. This Latin Patrology (usually cited as "PL"), containing all the works of the Latin ecclesiastical writers from the second century through the twelfth century, is the fundamental source book for all studies of early medieval philosophy. There is also a Greek Patrology ("PG"), containing the Greek ecclesiastical writers from the first century to the fifteenth century, together with Latin translations.

Corpus scriptorum ecclesiasticorum Latinorum. Vienna, 1866–1942. 70 volumes published so far. This Vienna Corpus (usually cited as "CSEL"), containing critical editions of selected works of the Latin Fathers, is to be preferred to the Latin Patrology for the works which it includes.

Rauschen, G., P. B. Albers, B. Geyer, and J. Zellinger (editors). Florilegium patristicum. Bonn, 1911–1938. 43 fascicles published so far. This collection contains critical editions of selected works of Latin (and some Greek) patristic and medieval writers.

Baeumker, C., and M. Grabmann (editors). Beiträge zur Geschichte der Philosophie und Theologie des Mittelalters. Münster, 1891–1939. 35 volumes published so far. This collection contains both critical texts of selected works and scholarly researches on various problems in the field of medieval philosophy and theology.

Gilson, Étienne (editor). Études de philosophie médiévale. Paris, 1922–1947. 35 volumes published so far. This collection contains monographs on various patristic and medieval philosophers, together with some critical texts and special researches.

Vacant, A., E. Mangenot, and É. Amann (editors). Dictionnaire de théologie catholique. Paris, 1903–1949. 15 volumes published so far, including alphabetically arranged articles from A to W. Has excellent encyclopedic articles on authors and subjects in medieval philosophy.

McKeon, Richard (editor and translator). Selections from Medieval Philosophers. New York, 1929. 2 volumes. Literal English translations of selected passages on the theory of knowledge from medieval philosophers, with brief introductions.

Geyer, Bernhard (editor). Friedrich Ueberwegs Grundriss der Geschichte der Philosophie. Part II: Die patristische und scholastische Philosophie. 11th edition. Berlin, 1928. The standard reference history of medieval philosophy.

Wulf, Maurice de. Histoire de la philosophie médiévale. 6th edition. Louvain, 1934–1947. 3 volumes. A history of medieval philosophy more readable than Ueberweg-Geyer, and including later bibliographical references. (The student should be sure to use the latest edition.) There is an English translation of Volumes I and II by E. C. Messenger: History of Mediaeval Philosophy, 3d English edition based on the 6th French edition, London, 1935–1938.

Gilson, Étienne. La Philosophie au moyen âge. 2d edition. Paris, 1944. A scholarly work in a popular style.

—— and P. Böhner. Die Geschichte der christlichen Philosophie. Paderborn, 1937. A textbook of Christian philosophy from the first century to the fifteenth century.

## JOHN SCOTUS ERIGENA

### Text

Migne, J. P. (editor). Latin Patrology. Volume CXXII contains Erigena's complete works.

### Translation

Division of Nature, Book IV, chapters vii-ix. McKeon, Richard (editor and translator), Selections from Medieval Philosophers, I, pp. 106–141.

### Biography

Cappuyns, Maïeul. Jean Scot Érigène, sa vie, son œuvre, sa pensée. Louvain, 1933. Contains a bibliography.

### Expositions

Schneider, Artur. Die Erkenntnislehre des Johannes Eriugena. Berlin and Leipzig, 1921–1923. 2 volumes.

Bett, Henry. Johannes Scotus Erigena, a Study in Mediaeval Philosophy. Cambridge, England, 1925.

## ANSELM OF CANTERBURY

### Texts

Migne, J. P. (editor). Latin Patrology. Volumes CLVIII and CLIX contain Anselm's complete works.

Opera omnia, edited by F. S. Schmitt. 6 volumes. Volume I (Seckau, 1938; reprinted Edinburgh, 1946), works written as prior and abbot. Volume II (Rome, 1940), works written as archbishop. Volume III (Edinburgh, 1946), prayers, meditations, and 147 letters. Volumes IV, V, and VI (not yet published), letters and fragments.

Florilegium patristicum. Includes Cur Deus homo (fascicle 18), Monologion (fascicle 20), De incarnatione Verbi [commonly called De fide Trinitatis] (fascicle 28), and Proslogion, with Gaunilon's objection and Anselm's reply (fascicle 29).

Cur Deus homo. Erlangen, 1834. Berlin, 1857. Zurich, 1868. London, 1886. Prima forma inedita, edited by E. Druwé, Analecta Gregoriana, Volume III, Rome, 1933.

De potestate et impotentia, possibilitate et impossibilitate, necessitate et libertate. Schmitt, F. S. (editor), Ein neues unvollendetes Werk des hl. Anselm von Canterbury (Beiträge zur Geschichte der Philosophie und Theologie des Mittelalters, XXXIII, 3), pp. 23-45.

## Translations

Deane, S. N. (translator). St. Anselm. Chicago, 1903. Contains Monologion, Proslogion (with objection and reply), and Cur Deus homo.

Cur Deus homo, translated by a clergyman. 3d edition. Oxford, 1868.

Dialogue on Truth. McKeon, Richard (editor and translator), Selections from Medieval Philosophers, I, pp. 150-184.

## Biographies

Rule, Martin. The Life and Times of St. Anselm. London, 1883. 2 volumes.

Ragey, P. Histoire de saint Anselme. Paris, 1889. 2 volumes.

Rigg, J. M. St. Anselm of Canterbury. London, 1896.

## Exposition

Filliatre, Charles. La Philosophie de saint Anselme. Paris, 1920.

## PETER ABELARD

### Texts

Cousin, Victor (editor). Ouvrages inédits d'Abélard. Paris, 1836. Contains Cousin's Introduction, the Sic et non, the Dialectic, the anonymous De generibus et speciebus, and certain minor works.

—— (editor). Petri Abaelardi opera. Paris, 1849–1859. 2 volumes. Contains the letters (including the Story of Calamities), the poetical works, the sermons, the Introduction to Theology, the commentary on Romans, the Christian Theology, the Scito teipsum, the dialogue, and certain minor works. This edition is to be preferred to that of the Latin Patrology.

Migne, J. P. (editor). Latin Patrology. Volume CLXXVIII contains the letters (including the Story of Calamities), the sermons, the Scito teipsum, the commentaries on the Six Days and on Romans, the Introduction to Theology, the Christian Theology, the Sic et non, the dialogue, the poetical works, and certain minor works.

Geyer, Bernhard (editor). Peter Abaelards philosophische Schriften. Beiträge zur Geschichte der Philosophie und Theologie des Mittelalters, XXI: i. Die Logica "Ingredientibus," nos. 1 (gloss on Porphyry), 2 (gloss on Categories), 3 (gloss on De interpretatione). ii. Die Logica "Nostrorum petitioni sociorum," no. 4.

Ostlender, Heinrich (editor). Peter Abaelards Theologia "Summi boni" [commonly called De unitate et trinitate divina]. Beiträge zur Geschichte der Philosophie und Theologie des Mittelalters, XXXV, 2–3.

### Translations

Bellows, H. A. (translator). Historia calamitatum, the Story of My Misfortunes. St. Paul, 1922.

Moncrieff, C. K. S. (translator). The Letters of Abelard and Heloise. London, 1925; New York, 1926. There are also other translations of the letters (including the Story of Calamities).

McKeon, Richard (editor and translator). Logic "Ingredientibus," the gloss on Porphyry (selection). Selections from Medieval Philosophers, I, pp. 208–258. This selection includes Abelard's discussion of the problem of universals.

McCallum, J. R. (translator). Abailard's Ethics. Oxford, 1935. A translation of Scito teipsum.

### Biography

Sikes, J. G. Peter Abailard. Cambridge, England, 1932. Contains a bibliography.

# BERNARD OF CLAIRVAUX

## Texts

Opera omnia, edited by Jean Mabillon. Paris, 1667; 4th edition, 1839. 2 volumes in 4 parts. There are several editions of this text, and it is included in the Latin Patrology, Volumes CLXXXII (letters and essays), CLXXXIII (sermons), CLXXXIV, CLXXXV.

Sermones de tempore, de sanctis, de diversis. Xenia Bernardina, Part I. Vienna, 1891. Contains all the sermons except those on Canticles. This is the best edition, but does not differ substantially from Mabillon's.

Select Treatises of S. Bernard of Clairvaux. Cambridge, England, 1926. Contains critical texts of the essays on Loving God (edited by W. W. Williams) and the Steps of Humility (edited by B. R. V. Mills).

## Translations

Eales, S. J. (translator). Life and Works of Saint Bernard. London, 1889–1896. 4 volumes published. Contains the letters, the essay on Abelard's Errors, the first 19 sermons De tempore, and the sermons on Canticles.

Works, translated by a priest of Mount Melleray. Dublin, 1920–1925. 6 volumes published. Contains the sermons and the essay on Consideration. This translation of the sermons on Canticles is to be preferred to that of Eales.

Lewis, George (translator). Saint Bernard on Consideration. Oxford, 1908.

Williams, Watkin (editor and translator). Of Conversion. London, 1938. Includes a critical text.

Mills, B. R. V. (translator). The Twelve Degrees of Humility and Pride. London, 1929.

Burch, G. B. (translator). The Steps of Humility. Cambridge, Mass., 1940. Includes the text and an analysis of Bernard's theory of knowledge.

Gardner, E. G. (translator). The Book of Saint Bernard on the Love of God. London, 1915. Includes the text.

Connolly, T. L. (translator). The Book of Saint Bernard on the Love of God. New York, 1937.

Williams, W. W. (translator). Concerning Grace and Free Will. London, 1920.

### Biographies

Vacandard, E. Vie de saint Bernard. Paris, 1894; 8th printing, 1927. 2 volumes. The best biography.

Luddy, A. J. Life and Teachings of St. Bernard. Dublin, 1927. Emphasizes Bernard's doctrine.

Williams, Watkin. Saint Bernard of Clairvaux. Manchester, 1935. Emphasizes Bernard's political activities.

### Exposition

Gilson, É. La Théologie mystique de saint Bernard. Paris, 1934. Contains a bibliography. There is an English translation by

A. H. C. Downes: The Mystical Theology of Saint Bernard, New York, 1940.

## ISAAC OF STELLA

### Text

Migne, J. P. (editor). Latin Patrology. Volume CXCIV contains Isaac's complete works.

### Biography

Bliemetzrieder, F. P. "Isaak von Stella: Beiträge zur Lebensbeschreibung," *Jahrbuch für Philosophie und spekulative Theologie,* XVIII (1904), 1–34.

### Expositions

Bliemetzrieder, F. P. "Isaac de Stella: sa spéculation théologique," *Recherches de théologie ancienne et médiévale,* IV (1932), 134–159.

Meuser, W. Die Erkenntnislehre des Isaak von Stella. Bottrop, 1934.

# INDEX